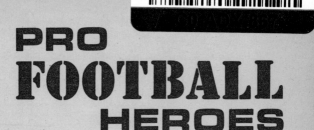

PRO FOOTBALL HEROES

by STEVE GELMAN

Illustrated with photographs

Cover photograph by Tony Tomsic
for Sport Magazine

SCHOLASTIC BOOK SERVICES
New York Toronto London Auckland Sydney

For Mitchell and Jan

Other books by the same author
available through
Scholastic Book Services:

YOUNG OLYMPIC CHAMPIONS
YOUNG BASEBALL CHAMPIONS

4th printing..................................September 1970

Printed in the U.S.A.

Contents

Quarterback Johnny Unitas (No. 19) fades back in the pocket, looking for a receiver. His passing skills and leadership have made him pro football's number one quarterback since 1958.

The Quarterback Who Never Quits

HE stood out on the highway, trying to hitchhike home. Yesterday Johnny Unitas had been a rookie quarterback with the Pittsburgh Steelers, and he was looking forward to a fine future in pro football. Today Johnny had no job and his future was uncertain. A few minutes ago the Pittsburgh coach had called him in for a conference.

The other fellows who had tried out at quarterback in the training camp had played better than Johnny, the coach had said. The Steelers couldn't keep everybody, so they would have to let him go.

The Steelers had given Unitas bus fare to get from their Olean, New York, training camp to his home in Pittsburgh, Pennsylvania. But Johnny decided he'd better hitchhike and save the money. He had a wife and baby to support, and now, without a job, he'd be needing every penny.

When Johnny got home to Pittsburgh, he sat down and thought very seriously about his future. He was twenty-two years old this late summer day in 1955, and for as long as he could remember he had wanted to be a pro football quarterback. He knew he was good, too. He had been a star at Louisville University, and when he'd graduated a few months ago the Steelers had selected him in the National Football League draft. Now he felt that the Steelers hadn't let him prove just how good he was. Perhaps another pro football team *would*.

Johnny decided to take a chance. He sent a telegram to Paul Brown, coach of the Cleveland Browns, and asked for a tryout. Brown wired back that it was too late, that the season was about to start, but he'd be glad to take a look at Johnny in next summer's training camp. At least, thought Johnny, it was something to look forward to.

Convinced now that he couldn't get into pro football until the next year, Johnny took a job as a pile driver on a construction gang. Meanwhile, to stay in shape for his next pro football tryout, he began playing with a semipro team, the Bloomfield Rams.

The Rams played every Thursday night at the Arsenal Street School playground in the Bloomfield section of Pittsburgh. The field was covered with stones, and there wasn't any grass on it at all. A few hundred people might show up to watch the games, but more often it was less than a hundred. For playing quarterback with the Rams in those games, Johnny was paid six dollars every Thursday night. He gave this money to his wife to spend on things she wanted — not just necessities. The family was living on a very tight budget then, and Johnny's wife has said since that "No money I ever get will ever seem quite so large to me as that six dollars."

Throughout that season with the Bloomfield Rams, people often asked Johnny what he was going to do in the future. His reply was always the same: he was going to play quarterback in the National Football League.

"The guys used to kid him about it," says one of his teammates. "He was the best ballplayer in our league, and everyone knew it, but still it didn't seem to make sense for a guy playing sandlot ball to be talking about signing with the Cleveland Browns. Sometimes they would needle him. 'Hey,' some guy would yell, 'did you hear about me, Unitas? The Chicago Bears want me.' But they didn't bother Johnny any. He kept his mouth shut and played the game. You had to admire him."

In February, a phone call finally came through for Johnny from a pro football team. But not from the Browns. From the Baltimore Colts. Don Kellett, the Colts' general manager, asked Johnny if he would like to come to Baltimore in May and go through a light workout for coach Weeb Ewbank. If Ewbank liked what he saw, Kellett said, Johnny would be invited to join the team in the regular camp in July. Johnny naturally said he'd be there.

How did the Colts happen to call Johnny Unitas? No one knows exactly. Two different stories have been sworn to through the years — one by Kellett, the other by Ewbank. Kellett insists that he was looking over some old waiver lists — lists of players released by other NFL teams — when he came across Johnny's name. "I remembered that he had been a high Pittsburgh choice," Kellett's version goes. "We had scouted him ourselves, and I believe had him down as a late draft choice if he was still eligible. We were on the lookout for a quarterback because Gary Kerkorian had already announced he was going to give up football. Any time you can pick up a quarterback for nothing, you grab him."

Ewbank has always insisted that there *was* no old waiver list. "That is a made-up story," goes Ewbank's version. "Unitas was

signed after we received a letter from a fan
— addressed to the club, not to me — telling
us there was a player in Bloomfield deserv-
ing a chance. I always accuse Johnny of writing it."

Johnny didn't care how the Colts had discovered him. What he cared about was getting to Baltimore and showing them how he
could fire a football. He went down there on a
spring weekend. Ewbank was really impressed with the power and accuracy of Johnny's passes and the strength in his six-foot,
one-inch, 196-pound body. "He was a big boy
with a good arm and good speed," Ewbank
has said. "And he was so very eager to learn.
I liked that, and I liked his size."

Unitas was given a seven-thousand-dollar
contract and invited to training camp. There
he won a place on the 1956 Colts, beginning
the season as quarterback George Shaw's
substitute and ending it, after an injury to
Shaw, as the number one quarterback. He
remained number one quarterback in 1957,
and then his superstar skill started flashing.
Johnny completed 57.1 per cent of his passes
in '57 for a whopping 2,550 yards and 24
touchdowns, only four short of the NFL record. With Unitas leading them, the Colts
were third in the Western Conference, their
highest finish ever.

The next year Johnny led the Colts to victories in their first six games. But in that sixth game a Green Bay linebacker cracked him so hard that three of Johnny's ribs were broken and a lung was punctured. He was hospitalized, and it looked as though he would be lost for the rest of the season. But after a week's rest, he insisted upon trying to play.

He reported to practice wearing an aluminum corset to protect his ribs, and found he could throw without too much pain. In fact, Johnny sat out only two games — one of them a loss to the New York Giants — then he came back. Pumping his passes expertly and calling plays with skill and guile, he led the Colts to the Western Conference championship. Even though he'd missed two games, he'd still gained more than 2,000 yards with his passes, and thrown for 19 touchdowns.

The Colts met the Giants for the championship, and it was probably the most dramatic game ever played. With two minutes left and New York ahead 17–14, Baltimore had the ball on its own 14-yard line. "Okay," Johnny said in the huddle. "We've got some 80 yards to go and two minutes to do it in. Now we find out what stuff we're made of."

They found out fast. Blending some key

running plays in with his passes, Johnny began to move the Colts. Quickly they marched up the field. The most critical gains came on three passes from Johnny to end Raymond Berry; they ate up 62 yards. Then, with seven seconds remaining, Steve Myhra kicked a field goal to tie the game.

Now it was sudden death, an overtime, the first in NFL history. The first team to score would be the winner, the champion of pro football. Anything — a field goal, a touchdown, a safety — would win the game.

The Colts kicked off, then stopped the Giants and forced them to punt. Taking over on his own 20, Unitas sent halfback L. G. Dupre around right end for 10 yards, then, after an incompleted pass, sent Dupre into the middle for three yards. Dropping back to pass on the next down, Johnny searched the secondary for Berry. Raymond was covered, but Johnny picked out the form of fullback Alan Ameche cutting across the 40. Instantly Johnny whipped the ball into Ameche's gut, and the Colts had another first down.

Now it was Dupre again, Johnny handing off to the halfback and watching him gain seven. After that a 12-yard loss and, for the Colts, third down and 15 to go. Backpedaling to throw, Johnny saw Carl Karilivacz, the man covering Berry, fall down. Berry cut to the sidelines unaware that his defender had fallen. Even more important, Berry hadn't gone deep enough; he was some yards short of the first down. Coolly, Johnny stood back, holding the ball, and waved to Berry to go deeper. At the last instant, as the Giants swarmed him, Johnny threw the ball to Berry for a first down on the Giant 42.

As he hunched over the center on the next play, Johnny noticed the Giant middle linebacker, Sam Huff, drop back a few yards and slide to the side to help out on pass coverage. Johnny had called a pass play in the huddle, but now, at the line of scrimmage, he barked out signals for a new play. Instead of passing, he handed off to fullback Ameche, who raced right in the hole that Huff had left open. Ameche charged up the middle for 23 yards.

Two passes, one to Berry and the other to Jim Mutscheller, brought the ball to the Giant one-yard line, then Johnny called upon Ameche again. Johnny slapped the ball in the big fullback's belly, and Ameche blasted into the end zone. The Colts were world champions, and Johnny Unitas, who only three years earlier had been playing sandlot football for six dollars a game, was the most celebrated star in pro football.

Unitas brought the Colts another world championship in 1959, and for eight years after that, although the best he could get them was one more Western Conference title, he remained the number one quarterback in the league. In all, from his first season, 1956, through 1967, he completed the most passes in pro football history (2,261) for the most yards (33,022) and the most touchdowns (252). He set another record by throwing at least one touchdown pass in 47 consecutive games.

His success was based on more than his strong throwing arm. It was built upon his faking — his knack of looking at one man and throwing to another, of shoving the ball into the stomach of one runner and then pulling it out and handing off to another. It rested on his dazzling play selection — his ability to mix up opponents by calling unexpected plays, his skill at inspecting defenses at the line of scrimmage and then, as he did against the Giants in '58, switching plays at the last minute. And largely it was based on his leadership.

"The quarterback has to be in charge out there," Johnny once explained. "If he doesn't have confidence in what he's doing, and if the coach doesn't have confidence in him, he isn't going to be able to do the job. I take a few

plays from the coach into the game for the
very first series. After that I'm on my own."

Early in his football career, Johnny had
demonstrated his talent at taking charge. As
a freshman quarterback for Louisville University, he had moved his team to the Hous-
ton University 40-yard line late in the fourth
quarter. The score was 21–21, and Louisville
had a fourth down coming with two yards to
go for a first. In the huddle, a veteran fullback snapped, "Give me the ball. I'll get the
two yards for you." Johnny stared at the
veteran and said, "When I want you to take
it, I'll tell you," then called a pass and threw
for a touchdown.

But there is more to leadership than simply ordering players around, and Johnny always demonstrated the necessary supporting
qualities. First, he shared the credit, talking
time and again about how he could never
have thrown those touchdown passes without the protection of his big Baltimore
blockers — men like Jim Parker and Alex
Sandusky. And he always knew how to build
up the confidence of the men he played with.
In 1967, in a critical game against the Los
Angeles Rams, Johnny threw a fourth-down
pass to a rookie end, Ray Perkins, who was
free in the end zone. The ball floated in per-
fectly, Perkins grabbed it, then dropped it,

and the Rams took over and scored a touchdown. "Perkins was shaken," columnist Joe Falls later wrote. "But not Unitas. In his very next offensive play he threw the ball right back to the rookie, to let him know he was still part of the team."

Johnny earned the respect of his teammates by respecting *them*, and by showing them that he was always cool and confident no matter how much pressure was upon him.

"If Unitas completes a pass, or if he has one intercepted," a Colt executive once said, "he comes off the field looking the same. If you hadn't seen the play, you couldn't tell from his expression whether he'd thrown a touchdown pass or fumbled."

One of the things that helped Johnny as he piled up his records was his skill at injecting this confidence into his teammates. In 1964, the day before the Colts were to play the Cleveland Browns for the NFL championship, Johnny and the team went out to the Cleveland Stadium for a workout. "At the stadium," John Devaney has written, "the Colts got off their buses and walked through the stone gates of the huge, cavernous arena. They walked up a ramp into the lower grandstand and stared out at the empty tarpaulin-covered field.

"There was a long silence, maybe for ten

seconds, each player perhaps wondering
what he would find on this field twenty-four
hours hence. Then Unitas, who had been one
of the last to leave the bus, came up the ramp.
On tiptoe he poked his burr [crewcut] head
over the knot of players to see what they
were looking at.

" 'Hey,' he yelled, 'haven't any of you ever
seen a football field before?'

"Gino Marchetti, standing next to Unitas,
laughed, and then the other Colts began to
laugh, a little embarrassed. 'A football field
is one-hundred-and-twenty yards long,'
Unitas was barking, turning his back and
walking down the ramp. 'And it's about fifty
yards wide, and it's got goalposts . . .'

"His words were drowned out by the
shouts of the other Colts. Loose and laughing, they followed Unitas and Marchetti
down the ramp to the clubhouse."

Johnny learned early in life the value of
staying confident and cool. "The things I've
done," he once said. "Well, they're nothing
to be so proud of when you look at what my
mother did."

Johnny was very proud of his mother. She
had managed to care for and support her four
small children all by herself after Johnny's
father died. She took over her husband's
coal-delivery service and actually drove the

coal truck. Johnny and his brother helped her to load and unload it. At night, when the children were sleeping, Mrs. Unitas worked as a scrubwoman in office buildings downtown. Besides doing all this, she was going to business school to study bookkeeping, and before long she was working as a bookkeeper for the city of Pittsburgh.

Meanwhile Johnny was growing up and getting more and more interested in sports. At St. Justin's high school he played varsity basketball as well as football. Then, after being turned down by a Notre Dame coach who thought he was too skinny to ever make it in college football, Johnny had accepted his scholarship to Louisville. From there he moved into pro football — first as rookie with the Steelers, then with the Bloomfield Rams, and finally with the Baltimore Colts, where his skill and determination impressed everyone. Johnny's teammate Alex Hawkins spoke for all the team when he said one day, "How can you ever give up when you have Unitas going for you? As long as we have *that* guy, I'll never believe we're out of any game — any game at all — until it's over."

Modern Iron Man

CHUCK Bednarik always would remember the first football he ever owned. It wasn't a real football. His father worked hard in the steel mills to feed and clothe six children, and there was no money left over for fancy toys. But Chuck learned early that all you needed was a little imagination; then you could have as much fun as the rich kids.

Chuck's football was a sock — a plain old sock that you wear on your foot. He would stuff the sock with rags or leaves, then he and his friends would scramble over the barbed-wire fence surrounding the athletic field of a nearby college. There they would pass the stuffed sock, and catch it, and run with it, and kick it. After a while, caught up in the excitement of their game, they would forget they weren't playing with a real football. You tackled a halfback the same way whether he was running with a leather ball or a stuffed sock, and you blocked the same, and a touchdown still counted six points, and you still felt happy when your team won and sad when it lost.

Chuck's team usually won. Even back in 1936 when he was eleven, he was an excellent player. He was tall, lean, strong, and fast, and he was a punishing blocker and tackler. When Chuck Bednarik lowered his head, tucked in his chin, rammed first his shoulder and then his body into an opponent, that boy would spring backward as if swatted by an elephant's trunk.

Chuck could kick a football high and far, too. He loved kicking as much as he loved blocking and tackling. His father spent months one year saving up twenty-five coffee bags, then turned them in at the grocery store for a special prize: a real football! The day Chuck got the football he went out on the field and kicked it hundreds of times. Within weeks the football had been kicked so much it was raggedy and torn. Chuck kept kicking it until he couldn't use it any more, then saved the pieces as a souvenir.

Through elementary school and into junior high school in Bethlehem, Pennsylvania, Chuck was like the other boys in his neighborhood. He attended classes, did his homework, took on part-time jobs, played games.

But in neighborhoods where families don't have much money, children grow up fast. While he was still in junior high, Chuck decided that he was big enough to start taking on adult responsibilities. He went to his junior high football coach and said he thought it was time for him to quit school. "I'll go out and get a job," Chuck said. "I can work at the mills and make money to help out my family."

The coach said no, he didn't think that was a good idea. "You'll be in high school next year," he said, "and you'll be good enough to play for the varsity right away. If you play well and do well in the classroom, you'll have a chance to get a football scholarship to college. Sure, you can go out and make some money now. But if you go to college, someday you'll be able to make lots of money — lots more than you'd be making in the mills in ten years."

Chuck thought about that, and it made sense. He finished the year in junior high, then went on to Bethlehem High School. After a few days in high school, he told his parents he was going to try out for the football team. "But first," he said, "you have to sign this paper, giving me permission to play."

"No," said his mother. "You can get hurt."

Chuck couldn't believe it. He'd been play-

ing football since he'd been big enough to
know what a touchdown was. Of course he
hadn't ever played against boys as big and
as tough as those on the high school teams,
but he was big and strong, and pretty tough
too. He asked again, and again his mother
said no. Then he asked a third time.

"Look," said his father. "The boy wants
to play." Then he turned to Chuck, saying,
"I'm still the boss here. You go play."

At his first practice Chuck was standing at
one end of the field, punting — "punting the
livin' stuffing out of the ball," he told a
friend later. As he punted, he kept glancing
over to his new coach, Jack Butler, to see if
the coach was watching. Finally, after one
booming punt, he saw the coach stare at him
and begin marching over. In an instant the
coach was at Chuck's side, inspecting him
from helmet to cleats. "You look like a fullback," the coach said. "Do you want to play
there?" Chuck nodded his head furiously.
Fullback was a fine position to play. Any position was fine.

Chuck began working out at fullback with
the first string. But before the season opener
Bethlehem High lost its starting center.
Coach Butler had other fullbacks, but no other center, so he asked Chuck if he'd ever
played center. "No," Chuck said.

"Here's a football," Coach Butler said. "Take it home over the weekend and you'll be a center on Monday."

Chuck took the ball home, practiced with it, and was first-team center for Bethlehem from then on. "He was a great blocker on offense," Coach Butler once said. "And on defense, well, he was absolutely sensational. He loved to go after that ball carrier and bowl him over, and he was quick enough to get back on passing plays to break them up or intercept."

By the end of his senior year Chuck clearly was good enough to play college football. A number of colleges were offering him scholarships. But the country was at war — World War II — and Chuck went straight into the Air Force. Serving as a bomber waistgunner in a B-24, he flew twenty missions over Germany. Often Sergeant Bednarik's plane returned to its base in London with 120 or 130 flak holes. Sometimes an engine was shot out too.

In the spring of 1945, after his last mission, Chuck leaped out and kissed the plane. When he came home to Bethlehem he proudly wore an Air Medal, five battle stars, and five oak-leaf clusters.

Chuck was twenty years old then, and he hadn't forgotten his ambition. He visited his old high school coach, Coach Butler, and said, "I'd like to play football at college."

"Fine," Butler said. "Let me call Coach George Munger at the University of Pennsylvania."

Chuck stood by as Butler dialed. Then, after what seemed like an hour, he heard the coach say, "I think I've got a football player for you."

Chuck could not hear Munger ask, "Where's he play?" But he did hear Butler say, "Center."

Suddenly Chuck saw Butler frown. On the other end of the line Munger was saying, "I've got *five* centers, including the team captain. I don't need another."

"Listen," said Butler, "I don't care how many you have. This fellow's six one and 205 pounds. He can center a football, kick it a mile, and he blocks and tackles like a pro."

Then Butler began to grin. Munger's answer had been precise and perfect: "Send him along."

Chuck enrolled at Penn, moved right into the first team, and played his first game a week later, against Princeton. In his next game, against Columbia, he was the defensive hero, making so many tackles that the students began calling him "The Clutch." They loved the way he swept in from his po-

sition backing up the line, banged into a ball
carrier, enveloped him with his long arms and
thick hands, and wrestled him to the ground.

Chuck punted for Penn too, and sometimes
ran or passed from punt formation. He ran
so well, smashing straight ahead with power and sprinting the ends with long, loose
strides, that Munger said, "If he wasn't the
best center and linebacker I've ever seen, he
would make a great fullback. He could play
great end too, because he has the speed, the
size, and the strength."

Playing center and linebacker, Chuck led
the way for Penn's runners. He made 13 in-
terceptions in his first two seasons. And he
made, by one sportswriter's count, 50 to 60
per cent of Penn's tackles, and countless
game-saving plays.

One day Penn, leading Cornell by a touchdown, fumbled on its own 10-yard line. Cornell recovered, and in the stands Penn fans
moaned while Cornell fans began cheering
wildly. Cornell drove forward four times;
and four times, with Bednarik at or near the
bottom of the pile, Penn held. Presently Cornell had the ball again. With four minutes to
play, the ball was on the Penn 12, and again
the fans were roaring. Again it was up to
Bednarik. On the fourth down Cornell's
Norm Dawson swept around end toward the

goal line. At the three he ran into Chuck.
And the play ended right there.

Chuck played well in game after game.
The Columbia coach, Lou Little, said Chuck
was the best center he'd seen in twenty years.
His junior year, Bednarik was named the
nation's College Player of the Year by the
Maxwell Football Club, an organization
whose members were football experts. In
both his junior and senior years he was an
All-America. At the end of his college career
he was picked, along with Red Grange,
Ernie Nevers, and Don Hutson, as one of
the top eleven football players of the previous twenty-five years. Chuck was ready for
the pros.

The Philadelphia Eagles had first pick in
the NFL draft, and they passed up all the
available All-America backs. Instead, they
selected Chuck. By now he was 220 pounds
of solid muscle, and the Eagles felt he would
get even bigger and better.

Chuck had come to the pros with such a
record of success that he felt certain he would
begin starring immediately. But he didn't
even begin *playing* immediately. For one
thing, he was accustomed to centering the ball
from a single-wing formation, where the
tailback stood several yards behind him. Now
he had trouble adjusting to the Eagles' T-

formation, where the quarterback stood
inches behind him. In practice, Chuck would
snap the ball a distance of inches with the
same power he had once used to snap it several yards, and he all but mashed the fingers
of the Eagles' quarterbacks. He made other
mistakes as well. Through the early games
of his first season he sat on the bench.

Chuck was unaccustomed to being a bench-
warmer, and he went to see the Eagles'
coach, Greasy Neale. "I want to be traded,"
Chuck said. "My pride hurts when I sit on
the bench."

"Never mind your pride," Neale said.
"You're still getting paid."

But in the next game Neale let Chuck play
a few minutes. The coach used him at linebacker, and Chuck made tackles — and mistakes. A couple of times Chuck raced back
with a pass receiver, expecting the quarterback to throw; instead the quarterback sent
a runner blasting for big yardage into the
area Chuck should have been covering.

Chuck quickly realized that pro football
was tougher than any football he'd played
before. It was more exhausting, too. As the
season rolled on, he became very impressed
with the Eagles' big fullback, Jack Myers.
At various times Myers would play fullback
on offense, and stay right in the game to

play linebacker on defense too. Chuck used
to say to himself, "How does he do it? Sure,
I played both ways in college. But how does
he do it here, in the pros?"

Chuck played a few times as the Eagles
won the 1949 NFL championship, but mostly
he listened and learned. He learned well, and
by the end of 1950 he was an Eagle regular
and an NFL all-star as well. Playing center
in some games, but linebacker in most, Chuck
began carving the same kind of success in the
pros that he'd had in college. Beginning in
1951 he played in four straight Pro Bowl
games; in the fourth game he was voted the
Outstanding Player. He did all the punting
for the East that day. He made his usual
jarring tackles, and he scored a touchdown
on a 25-yard run with an intercepted pass.

Game after game, Chuck displayed his
versatile skills. Against the Baltimore Colts,
he swept out to cover a pass, intercepted it,
and ran it back 41 yards before he was tackled. Later in the game he picked off another
pass and sped 25 yards for a touchdown. He
was so delighted that time that he threw the
ball right over the stadium wall. A few minutes later he dropped back to punt, fumbled
the pass from center, fell down, scooped up
the ball, popped up, and still got away a 35-
yard kick. He also stopped so many of the

Colts' running plays that the next time the
two teams played each other Baltimore coach
Weeb Ewbank said, "We respect Bednarik so
much, we figure the best percentage is just
not to run his way."

But through the seasons, no matter how
well Chuck played, the Eagles could not put
together a championship team. Oh, the
Eagles had won in 1949, but Chuck hadn't
helped them much that year.

More than anything else, Chuck wanted to
star for a championship team. He stormed
along as the best linebacker in pro football,
and then, when he got a little older, he
switched to center and was honored as the
NFL's best at that position. But still no
championship. And at the end of the 1959
season, when Chuck announced his retirement, his ambition was unfulfilled.

Chuck was thirty-five years old then, and
he'd put in twelve seasons with the Eagles.
The team gave him a color television set and
a $1,000 bonus, and Chuck went to work as a
salesman for a concrete company. He was
pleased at the prospect of working regular
hours, of having so much more time at home
with his wife and four daughters. He looked
forward to the first summer in twelve years
that he'd be able to lie in the sun and swim,
instead of having to work out in the broiling

Chuck Bednarik races toward goal line with intercepted pass in 1954 NFL All-Star Game. He played center on offense and linebacker on defense for the Eagles.

heat of football training camp. But he knew
he'd miss the playing. You don't do something all your life and then just stop, without missing it.

Chuck also continued to think about that
championship, especially when he read about
new Eagle trades — player trades that would
really put the team in contention for the title. And so, at the end of the spring, when
the Eagles asked if perhaps he'd reconsider
and try it one more time, Chuck said yes he'd
try.

He began to prepare for the season. In the
two weeks before training camp, Chuck came
home early each night from his salesman's
job. At home he quickly changed into workout
clothes; then he and his family went down to
the high school athletic field. There the Bed-
nariks lined up and Chuck led them in calisthenics. Then he took some turns around the
running track, and after that he placed the
four girls and his wife at 10-yard intervals
along the field, so that he could practice punting and kicking. He boomed the ball as far
as 50 and 60 yards, and the family relayed
it back to him. Then he ran uphill a dozen or
so times in quick spurts. Since he had remained on his year-round athlete's diet, built
around broiled meats and green vegetables,
he hadn't become fat after his retirement,

so weight was no problem. When training camp began, he was ready.

The Eagles' 1960 coach, Buck Shaw, planned to use Chuck at center, and Chuck played that position in camp. But one day Eagle defensive coach Jerry Williams called him aside. "I'd like you to practice with the defensive unit once in a while," Williams said. "Just in case something happens."

Chuck continued to play center, but he practiced at linebacker too, and in the fifth game of the season — against the Cleveland Browns — something happened. Because of injuries, Philadelphia went into the game with only three linebackers, and on the first play one of them, Bob Pellegrini, was hurt. As Pellegrini was helped from the field, Shaw motioned to Bednarik. "Get in there, Chuck," Shaw said, "but don't pull any hero roles. If you get tired, tell me."

Chuck went in and, except for kickoff and punt returns, he never came out. He played linebacker and center for the rest of the game and the rest of the season. He was the first two-way pro player in years — a modern iron man.

With Chuck starring on offense and defense, and with quarterback Norm Van Brocklin firing touchdown passes to Tommy McDonald, the Eagles were driving toward

the Eastern Conference championship. But
the New York Giants were driving toward
that championship too, and in November the
two teams met in the season's most crucial
game.

Late in the fourth quarter, with Philadelphia ahead, the Giants got the ball for what
amounted to their last chance at victory.
Frank Gifford, the New York halfback, sped
out to the 30, stopped a split second to cut into an opening, and suddenly was flat on his
back — smashed to the ground by Chuck. He
was smashed so hard that he fumbled, and
the Eagles leaped on the ball, their victory
secure. A week later they beat the Giants
again and they had the Eastern Conference
title.

But that was only half the mission. To win
the NFL championship the Eagles now had
to beat the Western Conference winners, the
Green Bay Packers. They had to beat the
team that coach Vince Lombardi was building into the best ever to play pro football —
the team that starred Paul Hornung and
Bart Starr and Jim Taylor.

Chuck was always nervous before a football game. He would get up at seven thirty,
drink a cup of coffee and order some eggs, but
he was never able to eat them. He'd grab a
couple of chocolate bars, stuff them down for

energy, and then get out to the ball park early and say to himself, hundreds of times, "We have to win, we have to win." Before the Packer game, the biggest of his life, he was more nervous than he'd ever been. "Not *scared*," he said afterward. *"Nervous*. There's a big difference."

As always, though, once the game had begun, once he had crashed into an opponent for the first time, he was all right. Playing offense and defense, he helped the Eagles into the lead with his hard blocking, and he helped them protect it with his rough, sure tackling. It was a very rough game — a game against the Packers always is — and with ten seconds left, it still wasn't over. The Eagles were winning by four points, the sun was sinking behind Philadelphia's Franklin Field, and the Packers were in a huddle, shaping their strategy for the final play.

Chuck stood at the scrimmage line, the Eagle 20. His once-clean green-and-white uniform was smeared with dirt. Mud streaked his face. Quickly he moved up to each Eagle, giving individual orders. "Whatever you do," he said to each back, "get that end zone covered. Cover for the touchdown pass."

Green Bay put the ball into play. Quarterback Starr faded, looking into the end zone, but his receivers were covered. Finally, with the Eagle line charging, Starr got rid of the ball with a short pass to fullback Taylor.

Taylor exploded down the field, and Bednarik raced up to meet him. Ahead of him, Chuck saw his teammate, Don Burroughs, hit Taylor low and bounce off. Then he saw another teammate, Maxie Baughan, hit Taylor low and bounce off. "*I'm* not bouncing off," Chuck said to himself. "I'm bearhugging him high and I'm not bouncing off."

At the 10-yard line they collided — Bednarik struggling to hang on, Taylor squirming to break loose. The championship would be settled right there.

Chuck wrapped his arms around Taylor and squeezed. He twisted and knocked Taylor down, then slammed on top of the fullback and looked up at the clock. He watched the seconds tick off and watched the clock hit zero. Then he let go. "Okay, Taylor," he said. "You can get up now. This game is over."

In the locker room, amid the backslapping bedlam, Coach Shaw turned to the reporters. "We've got to thank the Old Pro," Shaw said, "and I mean Bednarik. He held us together on offense and defense."

Off to the side, Chuck Bednarik grinned and whooped. "There are other guys in this league who are *capable* of playing sixty minutes a game," Chuck said. "But I *did* it."

"He Could Lead His Own Interference"

THE New York Giants were due to play the Chicago Bears for the 1933 NFL championship when a reporter asked Giant coach Steve Owen the question on everybody's mind. "Steve," he said, "how will you stop Nagurski?"

Owen's answer was immediate: "With a shotgun, as he comes out of the dressing room."

It seemed the only way. Bronko Nagurski was six feet, one inch tall. He weighed 238 pounds. He was hard, trim, powerful. When he ran from fullback — head down, leather helmet driving at opponents, knees high, hard bone churning at them — it took mounds of muscle to stop him. Nagurski had to be gang-tackled. To expect one man to bring down Bronko was like expecting a mouse to bowl over an alley cat.

But if they were going to win this game,

the first title playoff in NFL history, the
Giants would have to throttle Nagurski.
They'd not only have to thwart his running,
but his passing too, because Bronko could
charge toward the line, stop suddenly, jump
up, and fire the ball with speed and accuracy.
They'd have to contend with him even when
the Bears didn't have the ball, because on defense too Bronko was always a threat. He
could slam a runner so hard he'd fumble.

There were 26,000 people in Wrigley Field
for the game that day. Almost all of them
were Bear fans, expecting victory and not
quite believing it when the first half ended
with the Giants ahead 7–6. Bronko had been
running well, and had set up the two Chicago field goals, but he still hadn't broken
loose.

Well into the third quarter, the Giants
were still leading, now by a 14–9 score. But
the Bears had the ball, and they weren't
panicking. They were going with the offensive tactic that had worked for them all season; it had brought them into the playoff
game. A simple tactic: Nagurski, straight
ahead. Time after time he tucked the ball under his arm, lowered his head, and charged
into the Giants. Slowly, gain by gain, he
moved the Bears upfield, and now they had
the ball on the Giant eight. The Bears lined

up, got the ball to Bronko, and he attacked. The Giants swept up to meet him, stacking at the line of scrimmage for the collision. Suddenly Bronko stopped, leaped up, and passed to Bill Karr in the end zone. The Bears had the lead.

The Giants came back. They scored in the fourth quarter to go ahead 21–16, and time was running short. Still the Bears didn't rush. It was line plunge after line plunge, Bronko carrying. Four times in a row he smashed into the center of the Giant line, those powerful knees driving, those big shoulders digging into opponents, and he brought the ball to the New York 36. Then he had the ball a fifth straight time and he was moving forward — three yards short of scrimmage, then two, then one. Abruptly he wasn't running low any longer; he was leaping and throwing — a perfect pass to Bill Hewitt on the 25. All the Giants but one, Ken Strong, had moved up to stop Bronko. Hewitt lateraled behind him to Karr, the Bear tackle Gene Ronzani blocked Strong, and Karr was free. He ran in for the touchdown that brought the Bears the championship.

Everyone, everywhere, who had any interest in football was in awe of Bronko. "There was something strange about tackling him," Red Grange once said. "When you

Bronko Nagurski (No. 3) blasts in for a Chicago Bear touchdown. "When you hit Bronko Nagurski," Red Grange once said, "it was like getting an electric shock."

hit him, it was like getting an electric shock."
And the writer Norman Katkov observed,
"When he was moving in his straightfor-
ward, terrifying way and someone came up
to hit him, the Bronk would not turn away.
He wouldn't even swerve a little. Out would
shoot his powerful arm, jamming into the
tackler's neck or head or shoulder, swift and
straight and painful. Then the Big Fellow
would follow through with his shoulders and
knees, running not over but absolutely
through the man."

Bronko was a rough man in a rough game.
"Pro ball was tough," he once said. "You had
eighteen men on the team back then. Maybe
less. Four of them are laid up. That's an average. Eleven are out there. That leaves four
substitutes. What substitutes? What positions? Say your left half — your runner —
is hit. In comes your substitute half. Now
your center is hit. But you got no substitute
center. So your guard takes center, your end
takes guard, and your blocking back on the
bench becomes end. If he gets hit, he stays
an end and stays in the game. There's nobody
to bail him out."

Bronko never needed anyone to bail him
out. Not on a football field anyway. Growing up in little towns in northern Minnesota,
he starred in sandlot and high school football

— always the number one man on any team
he played for. Then he went to Minneapolis
and enrolled at the University of Minnesota,
arriving there in September of 1926, a six-
foot, 218-pound eighteen-year-old alone in a
big school in a big city. He knew no one, and
he was shy and didn't make friends right
away, but he did know that he wanted to
play football. He showed up the first day that
the freshman team held tryouts. He lined
up at the tackling dummy and began to
watch the varsity team practicing across the
field. So engrossed was he that he didn't re-
alize his turn had come to hit the dummy.
"Hey," yelled the freshman coach, "hit that
dummy, dummy!" Bronko did.

"Hit it again," the coach yelled.

And Bronko did, knocking it — according
to the story people tell — right off its moor-
ings and 15 yards away.

Perhaps the story is a legend — many leg-
ends have sprung up about big Bronko —
but it's possible. Bronko was so big and
strong even then. Anyway, there he was, the
story goes, standing there with the whole
freshman squad and the freshman coach staring at him in wonder.

"What's your name?" the coach said.

"Bronko Nagurski."

"Your real name, kid."

"That's my real name. It's a Ukrainian name. I'm Ukrainian."

"Wait over there," the freshman coach said, walking away.

Moments later the freshman coach returned with the varsity coach, Doc Spears. "Where you from, boy?" Spears said.

Bronko told him.

"What position did you play?"

"Fullback," said Bronko. "Fullback and guard and tackle, and wherever they needed me."

Spears led Bronko to the varsity tackling dummy and asked him to hit it. Bronko slammed it hard and Spears smiled. Spears knew that the University of Minnesota had a remarkable new football player.

Bronko played freshman football, and played well, but he had other problems. After the season he went to the athletic equipment manager, Oscar Munson. "I'm going home," Bronko told him.

"Not until after finals," Munson said.

"I'm going home for good," Bronko said. "I haven't got money. I haven't got food money. My rent. I looked all over for a job. There isn't a job."

"You wait," Munson said, and walked away. Soon after that Bronko had a job tending furnace in an office building for fifty dollars a month.

Fifty dollars a month was enough to live on in those days, at least for a college student, and Bronko settled happily into school life, studying hard and waiting for the '27 season. When it came, he was first-team tackle in Minnesota's most important game of the year. Against Knute Rockne's heavily favored Notre Dame, Bronko showed the football world what he could do.

Early in the fourth quarter Notre Dame, ahead 7–0, lined up to punt. Back to do the punting, Ed Wynne grabbed the ball and, glancing up, saw Nagurski bursting through. Nagurski came crashing in, shoving aside blockers, arms and hands thrashing, head high. Wynne released the ball, swung his foot, and kicked. The ball thudded into Bronko, and instantly players were scrambling for it and piling upon each other.

In the stands, according to writer Katkov, the fans "went to their feet in a breathless hush and watched the officials unwind the package below them. They watched player after player come to his feet, but saw no ball until the last, the Big Fellow, rose, pigskin in hand, surrendering it gently to the referee." Then, with Bronko barreling out front to block, "it took Herb Joesting [the Min-

nesota fullback] four plays behind the Big
Fellow to score."

The game ended in a 7–7 tie, and Bronko
was headline news on sports pages all across
the country.

The next season Joesting had graduated.
Bronko played fullback and began impress-
ing people with his thundering style. "Bronko Nagurski," Grantland Rice wrote, "is the
only man who ever lived who could lead his
own interference in a game."

Against Iowa, Bronko ran over a man —
literally ran over him — to score a touchdown. While doing it Bronko cracked three
of his own ribs, and Spears said he'd be out
for a month. Bronko said no, he'd have trouble running with the ball, but he could do
other things, and the next week he played a
full game at tackle against Northwestern. A
few weeks after that he was back at fullback
against unbeaten Wisconsin, and at the half,
with the score 0–0, Spears told his squad,
"You're doing the best you can against a fine
team. I'm proud of you."

The score was still 0–0 in the fourth quarter when Wisconsin, on its own 20, shot a
runner through the line. Bronco swept up
and rammed a shoulder into the runner, hitting him so hard the ball popped into the air.
Bronko grabbed it, lowered his head, and

charged forward. He was hit at the 16, but brushed off the tackler. He was hit again at the 10, but broke free again. At the seven, two tacklers grabbed him and held on, but he dragged them along. At the five, a couple more caught hold, but he stormed forward anyway. At the two he was still moving, Wisconsin players draped all over him, and he dragged them all into the end zone.

"That was incredible," someone said to Bronko years later, "the way you carried five tacklers into the end zone against Wisconsin."

"Six," Bronko said quietly. "There were six."

After the season Spears said, "Aside from being the best tackle in the country, the best fullback in the Big Ten, a great guard, a fine halfback, and a remarkable end, Bronko isn't much of a football player at all."

In the next season, 1929, Bronko was equally incredible. He earned All-America acclaim and a pro contract with the Bears. Early in his first pro season, 1930, Chicago played the Green Bay Packers. In that game, whenever the Bears punted, Bronko and his teammate Red Grange lined up the same side as blockers. Grange was up close behind the line and Bronko was back deep, the last man between the opponents and the Chicago punt-

er. Time after time, when the Packers' big
tackle, Cal Hubbard, tried to get through,
Grange would knock him aside. Finally, late
in the game when the outcome was settled,
Hubbard asked a favor. "Red," he said,
"next time you kick, let me by. I won't block
it. I just want to get a shot at Nagurski. I've
been hearing how hard he is and I want a
crack at him."

Grange laughed and said sure, and the
next time the Bears punted he let big Hubbard through. Hubbard charged low and
hard and hit Bronko. And bounced straight
back. Catching up to Grange after the play,
Hubbard said simply, "That's enough."

Bronko was outstanding as a runner and
defender for the Bears through his rookie
season, and remained outstanding in the following years. His running and passing
brought the Bears the 1933 NFL championship.

In 1934 he became even more versatile. A
swift scatback, Beattie Feathers, joined the
club in 1934. To utilize Feathers' running
best, the Bears cut down on their use of the
T-formation. They began to work often from
a single wing, which was better suited to the
end sweeps that Feathers was so good at running. The success of these sweeps hinged
mostly on two players: the runner, Feathers;

and the blocker, Bronko, who led him out of the backfield and down the field. Throughout the season Feathers, in the words of one man, swung "in and out behind Bronko's shoulder blocks like a fox terrier frisking on the heels of a St. Bernard." Feathers gained 1,004 yards, a league record; the Bears won 12 straight games and the Western Conference championship.

In the '34 playoff against the Giants, Bronko ran for three touchdowns on a frozen field, but two were called back because of penalties. In the fourth quarter, with the Bears ahead and both teams slipping all over the ice, the Giants switched from cleats to sneakers, which gave them better traction. Able to run surefootedly while the Bears slid around, the Giants forged from behind to win.

Over the next few years Bronko continued thundering along at the pace that eventually gave him an NFL career total of 3,947 yards rushing and a career average of better than four and a half yards a carry. But before the Bears could win another NFL championship, he retired.

He returned to northern Minnesota to do the things he loved best — to farm and fish and hunt. He had never really enjoyed the big city, and he had no taste for fancy restaurants or night clubs or theaters. Now, with football behind him, he had no need to leave the woods and lakes he loved.

He lived that way for six years, until 1943. Then the Bears, who were shorthanded because most of their best players were in military service, asked him to come back. Bronko was thirty-five years old then, but he was still in good shape. He said okay. He played tackle through the season, a rousing tackle. But in the last game, which required a victory over the Chicago Cardinals to win the Western Conference title, coach Hunk Anderson asked Bronko if he'd move in at fullback if he was needed. In the fourth quarter, the Cardinals winning 21-14, Bronko *was* needed. He raced in and began plowing through the Cardinal line. In play after play, Bear quarterback Sid Luckman pushed the ball at Bronko's belly, and Bronko lowered his head and churned his knees and slammed through. Finally Bronko burst into the end zone with the football, and the Bears needed only one more touchdown to win.

Bronko returned to the bench, tired and sore, but the next time the Bears got the ball they needed him again. It was fourth down and four yards to go for a first down when Luckman *handed off* to his thirty-five-year-old fullback. Bronko got the Bears *six* yards. They went on to score and win.

The championship playoff was against the Washington Redskins. The year before, in the playoff, the Redskins and their great quarterback Sammy Baugh had beaten the Bears 14–6. And this time Washington went ahead 7–0 early in the second quarter.

The Bears scored on Luckman's touchdown pass, tying it, and soon had the ball again on their own 31. Bronko was in now — at fullback — and with Luckman throwing and Bronko running, the Bears moved toward the Washington goal. Presently they were on the Washington three and Bronko had the ball, plunging ahead, those big legs driving into the line. One Redskin hit him, then another, but he kept driving. Suddenly it was just like the old days. There was Bronko, charging on with opponents clinging to him, and then, with one big final burst, shaking loose and piling into the end zone.

Bronko had put the Bears ahead, and they never trailed again. Afterward, with the Bears the winners 41–21, Bronko sat in the locker room, his sides heaving, and announced, "I'm retiring again. And it's for keeps. It's not a game for thirty-five-year-old men."

Maybe not for most thirty-five-year-old men. But it was — that season — for Bronko Nagurski.

First of the Great Pro Pass Receivers

ALL the Chicago Bears were gunning for the Green Bay rookie. Coming into this opening game of the '35 season, the Bears had beaten the Packers seven straight times. Now, even though both teams had pretty much the same lineups as in '34, people were predicting Green Bay would win. The difference, they said, was the rookie — a new Packer, Don Hutson.

The Bears knew all about Hutson. He was a swift pass receiver who had been a sensation in the Rose Bowl back in January. "But that was college ball," one of the Bears said. "This is the National Football League. Sure, this Hutson can run fast. But in the pros that's not enough."

Don knew how the Bears felt about him, but he didn't say much before the game. In college he had sometimes talked it up on the

49

field, but mostly he was a quiet man. In a crowd he didn't chatter. During road trips he often sat off by himself thinking, while other players massed together for talk and horseplay. From the time he'd been a boy, he'd had a habit of avoiding groups and social gatherings, preferring to be alone or in the company of his family or one of his few close friends. Boys who don't always join in with the group are sometimes picked on, but Don proved to the people who knew him that there was nothing strange in being a quiet loner. When he had something he wanted to prove, he never boasted that he'd do it: he simply went out and did it.

Now Don had something to prove to the Bears. On the first play from scrimmage he lined up on the end, broke with the snap of the ball, and ran downfield, a defender right with him. They ran that way for about 20 yards, side by side, Hutson not breaking free. What the Bear defender did not know, however, was that while he was running full speed, Don was only coasting. Suddenly, Don burst into the open, looked back, fingertipped the football out of the air at the Chicago 35, and ran into the end zone.

Don won the game for Green Bay with that 65-yard touchdown play, and he continued breaking away from the Bears all afternoon. Afterward, with the final score 7–0, a big Bear tackle rushed up to him. "Okay," the tackle snarled, "but wait till next time." Don simply smiled.

Although he never bragged, Don Hutson knew just how good he was. And other people in the NFL found out fast. Before Don's first game against the Brooklyn Dodgers, the Brooklyn coach, Jock Sutherland, talked with some of the NFL coaches who had already played the Packers. They all told him how good Don was. Sutherland couldn't believe it. "You're telling me to put two or three men on Hutson?" he asked. "That's nonsense. No man can be that good." To reporters Sutherland said, "We aren't worried about Hutson. We're worried about the Green Bay defense."

The Green Bay defense proved every bit as tough as Sutherland had feared, and the toughest man was the Green Bay safety, Don Hutson. On offense, to Sutherland's amazement, Hutson was even better. He caught two touchdown passes, kicked four extra points, and ran away from the Dodger defense all day. "That man can run three ways at the same time," Sutherland said. "He's incredible."

Don was the first of the great pro pass receivers, and he could kick and play spectacular defense as well. In his ten-year NFL career, he caught 489 passes for 8,010 yards and 101 touchdowns. He led the league in scoring five times, and once he scored 29 points in a single quarter. He missed only one field-goal attempt, he never missed an extra point, and he left pro football owning or sharing a piece of nineteen records. And he did it all with a special flair.

Not having learned from Sutherland's lesson, Dutch Clark, coach of the Cleveland Rams, once put Dante Magnani on Hutson; he figured that one man *could* stop him. "Don't you dare let that guy get inside you," Clark said. "He won't," said Magnani. But Hutson did.

"On the first play," Larry Williams wrote in *Sport* Magazine, "Don loped down the field, magnificent stride in low gear. Magnani stuck with him like a hairshirt. The passer, Tony Canadeo, threw the ball toward the middle of the goalposts. Hutson shifted to second gear; Magnani stayed with him. They raced along, their backs to the soaring ball. Don suddenly picked up more speed, and Magnani ran faster; but as they sped abreast of the left upright, Hutson suddenly reached

Don Hutson grabs one of the 489 passes he caught in his NFL career. He was noted for his speed and for his skill at hauling in passes with defenders draped over him.

out, cocked his right wrist around the post,
swung around like an Arthur Murray dancer, and caught the ball as easily as you would
catch a February cold.

"It was sheer genius, an innovation of the
moment, a brilliantly improvised means to
an end. It was Don Hutson, the greatest pass
catcher of all time, doing what came naturally
and easily to him."

Curiously, for a man who had such sharp
athletic instincts, Don never cared much for
sports as a boy. Growing up in Pine Bluff,
Arkansas, he was more interested in rattle-
snakes than in anything else. He and his one
close friend, Bob Seawell, would spend hours
hunting snakes. Only when they grew tired
of the hunting would they play ball. When
they did play though, they were exceptionally good. In football Bob was a slick passer;
Don was of course a superb receiver. In baseball Bob could wallop long home runs. Don
could place hits expertly and, with his speed,
steal bases easily.

It was Bob who convinced Don to try out
for the high school football team, and it was
Bob who was the big star. Even as a senior
Don was only 145 pounds — too skinny to
attract much attention — and while Bob received many scholarship offers, Don received

none. But good friends look after each other, and when the University of Alabama offered him a scholarship Bob said, "You've got me if you take my friend Don Hutson too." Alabama agreed to take them both.

At Alabama, Bob drifted out of the athletic limelight and Don moved into it. And not only as a football player. "Don really had the irons in the fire," Bob remembered years later. "He went from one sport to another. The track coach and the baseball team had fusses about him. Don would run track in a sweatsuit, then go down to play centerfield for the baseball team. He was always working, but it was hard to tell it by just watching him. He made things look so easy compared to other athletes."

As good as he was in baseball — and that was good enough later to play three seasons with New York Yankee farm teams — football was where Don really excelled. He was an All-America end in 1934, catching the exquisite passes thrown by Millard (Dixie) Howell. Together, they led Alabama into the Rose Bowl and a memorable meeting with Stanford.

Stanford was ranked number one in the nation, but Alabama was not awed. Right away the Alabama players began razzing their opponents and moving the football against them. Once Stanford's Bobby Grayson flung a long low pass and Don tipped it, reached for it, but couldn't hold on because the ball had been thrown too close to the ground. "Hey, big boy," Hutson yelled at Grayson, "get your passes up. We can't catch them on the ground, and first bounce don't count in this league." Another time a Stanford end ran to the officials and complained about Alabama's roughness. "Shucks, Mr. Ref," said Hutson. "That's the way we play back home."

No one knows what prompted Don's outbursts; they were so untypical. But the other things that he did in the Rose Bowl were absolutely typical. All through the game he beat the Stanford defense to haul in Howell's passes, and Alabama so dominated the action that Don was able to sit out much of the fourth quarter. He was on the bench when Alabama got the ball with only minutes left and a 22–13 lead. Coach Frank Thomas, not wanting Stanford to get the ball again and not wishing to run up the score himself, turned to Don and said, "Get in there and tell Howell to lay off. Tell him to run out the clock. I don't want to see another pass."

Don ran in, but Howell called the play before Don could say a word. Naturally enough, Howell figured the coach had sent Don in for a long pass. That was the play he called.

Don sped down the field, Howell floated the ball to him, and Alabama had a 56-yard touchdown. "I had to catch it, Coach," Don said. "It was just too good a pass to drop."

After the game, on the train trip home, Don was sitting alone and staring out the window when a reporter came over and said, "How did it feel to catch all those passes before 87,000 people?"

"Well," said Don, "you run, and then you break away and you look over your shoulder and say, 'Hello, football, I've been expecting you,' and then you catch the ball."

"You mean," said the reporter, "that the ball is always there?"

"Yes," said Don. "Dixie Howell is the greatest passer in the world."

Howell himself, however, viewed the game another way. "Heck, fellers," he said. "All I did was rear back and throw. Hutson did the rest."

Don was now known nationally, and people were interested in his plans for the future. A rumor started that he wanted to become a movie actor. To those who didn't know

him it sounded reasonable, because he was
an exceptionally handsome man. But to Don,
shy and sports-loving, the idea was absurd.
"I'm an athlete, not an actor," he said.

"But I saw an acting class written in on
your school program," someone said.

"Acting nothing," Don said. "That's ac-
counting."

Curley Lambeau, coach of the Packers, was
keenly interested in Don's future. Before the
Rose Bowl game a number of pro scouts had
told Curley not to waste his time inspecting
Don. "They thought he was too skinny to
play pro ball," Curley later recalled. "But I
scaled a wall and watched a secret Alabama
practice before the Rose Bowl game to see
for myself. I didn't even have to watch the
Rose Bowl game itself. I was convinced right
there at that practice. Don would glide downfield, leaning forward as if to steady himself
close to the ground. Then, as suddenly as you
gulp or blink an eye, he'd feint one way, go
the other, reach up like a dancer, and grace-
fully squeeze the ball and leave the scene of
the accident — the accident being the defensive backs who tangled their feet up and fell
trying to cover him."

From that moment Curley had determined
to sign Don, and presently he did. So it was

on to the Packers for Hutson — to a second-place finish in the Western Conference in 1935 and the Conference championship in 1936. The '36 NFL championship too, because three minutes into the title playoff against the Redskins, Arnie Herber looked toward the end zone, waited for Don to break free, lobbed the ball to him for a 43-yard touchdown, and, with the conversion, those were all the points Green Bay needed. The Packers won 21–6.

Herber, the passer, was injured in 1937 and the Packers finished second. The next year with a new passer, Cecil Isbell, Green Bay won the Conference title. But Don was hurt and hobbling in the playoff, and the Giants beat the Packers 23–17.

Isbell and Hutson were back again in 1939, and although there was gossip that they weren't getting along personally, their teamwork didn't suffer. They worked together as well as any passing combination ever did. Even years later, when both had retired, they spoke of each other's skills in superlatives. "Isbell," Hutson said, "is the greatest passer Green Bay ever had." "Hutson," Isbell said, "was the first end with all the moves. He had good head and shoulder fakes, and he had an endless series of change of pace. It was impossible for one man to cover him, and almost impossible for two. He had absolute concentration on the ball. He never heard a footstep in his life, and he'd catch the ball in a crowd almost as easily as he did in the open. And he ran like a halfback after he got it."

Together Isbell and Hutson brought Green Bay the '39 championship, capped by a 27–0 win over the Giants in the playoff. Then "for the next four years," one man wrote, "the Packers had almost as good a team as the 1939 group. They had the misfortune, however, to be in the same division as the Chicago Bears, who had by then built their super-team. For four years the Packers could whip any team but the Bears, and for four years they finished second only to Chicago."

In one of those four years, 1942, Don set an NFL scoring record with 138 points on 17 touchdowns, 33 extra points, and one field goal; and he caught 74 passes for 1,211 yards. In the next, 1943, he was almost as good. Among his spectacular plays was an 83-yard touchdown run with an intercepted pass.

Then it was 1944 and Isbell was no longer playing football. A new young passer, Irv Comp, was throwing to Hutson. Comp threw well and Hutson, predictably, was sensational. Sensational enough to bring the Packers a division championship and a title showdown with the Giants.

It was a tough game, this last playoff Don would take part in before retiring to his lucrative businesses in 1946. The Packers had the ball and a 7–0 lead with seconds remaining in the first half. As usual, the Giants had been swarming around Hutson — two men, sometimes three, ranging out with him. But now Comp went to Don anyway — a high, hard pass thrown from the 50 to the Giant 26. Squeezing between defenders, Hutson grabbed the ball and there was time for one more play.

The Giants figured the last play had to be a pass to Hutson, and they stacked their coverage accordingly. At the beginning of his pro career, when teams challenged him with single coverage, Don had won ball games by easily outdistancing the one defender. These days teams were double-teaming and triple-teaming him, and now that was going to pay off for Green Bay too.

The ball was centered and Don swung out to his right. The Giant defense went with him, tugging at him, elbowing him, covering him front and back. As Don fought toward the corner, angling as far right as he

could, fullback Ted Fritsch slipped out of the
Packer backfield and sprinted down the *left*
sideline. The Giants were with Hutson; nobody was with Fritsch. Comp flipped the ball
to the fullback for the touchdown that made
the difference in the 14–7 final score. One way
or another, all the time he was with them the
Packers' victories were built upon the skills
of Don Hutson, who, in writer Williams'
words, "somehow managed to catch the
passes with three men hanging on him —
three men who had worked all week to make
sure that Hutson wouldn't catch the passes."

"Mr. Baugh Is Going to Pass Again"

DUTCH Meyer, the baseball coach at Texas Christian University, was on a scouting trip. Arriving at Abilene one steaming summer day, he was directed to a local ball park where he watched a tall, lean eighteen-year-old play third base. Meyer liked the way the boy scooped up grounders and belted line drives, and especially the speed with which the third baseman threw. Talking with him afterward, Meyer discovered that the boy had just graduated from high school and wanted to attend college, but had not yet enrolled at one. "I'll see what I can do," Meyer said, "about getting you a scholarship to TCU."

Back at the Texas Christian University's campus, Meyer went to the athletic director and head football coach. "I've found a real baseball player," Meyer said. "He fields well and hits the ball hard. I understand he plays a little football too."

The boy Meyer had discovered was Sammy Baugh. Today to say that Sammy played "a little" football is like saying Sandy Koufax was a "pretty good" pitcher. "Sammy Baugh," the sports historian Roger Treat once wrote, "played football for thirty years, sixteen of them in the fierce competition of the National Football League. The quality of his performance seldom varied; it was always good, sometimes incredible. In his worst games, with all the breaks going against him, he was as good as most quarterbacks are on their best days."

Sammy's specialty was passing. He was a great passer. One day when he was playing in college, the TCU center Ki Aldrich looked across at their opponents and said, "Gentlemen, Mr. Baugh is going to pass again. I don't know just where it'll go, but it'll be good. Ready!"

Whereupon Aldrich snapped the ball back, and Sammy flipped a perfect 25-yard pass to end Walter Roach. "Well now," Aldrich said, "I hate to be an old 'I-told-you-so,' but . . ."

Sammy could pass, and Sammy could punt, and Sammy could play defensive safety superbly. And yet none of it had come easily. His skills were developed with long, hard, boring practice.

Sammy grew up in Texas, where he was born on St. Patrick's Day in 1914. As a boy, Sammy spent whole afternoons working at a special passing drill he designed. He would hang an old automobile tire to a tree and begin by throwing the ball through the hole. Then he'd bang the tire so it would swing from side to side and, stepping back, he'd fire the ball through it. Finally, with the tire swinging, he'd throw the ball at it on the run, dodging from side to side, jumping in the air, falling back as if hit by a tackler. He'd loft the ball as he would later do when throwing over defenders to a receiver far downfield. He'd fire on a line as if this were a real game and his receiver stood 10 yards away, surrounded by opponents. He did all this day after day, and he became the star of the Sweetwater, Texas, high school football team.

Still, it was Sammy's baseball talent that earned him the scholarship of Texas Christian University. When he arrived there he said he'd like to play football too. Varsity coach Schmidt had his doubts. Sammy was six feet three inches tall, but he weighed only 170 pounds. Schmidt didn't believe that the skinny boy could survive in tough Southwest Conference football.

But Dutch Meyer, who had discovered
Sammy, didn't agree, and Meyer was freshman football coach as well as baseball coach.
He took one look at the way Sammy could
throw a football and decided that the boy
was even better at this sport than at baseball. All through Sammy's freshman football
season Meyer worked with him on passing
and punting, and kept telling him he was
going to be a star.

Then Schmidt retired as varsity coach, and
Meyer got the job. Sammy moved in as a
number one tailback, and by his junior year
he was shredding opponents with his precision passing and his booming punts. As a
junior he led TCU to the Sugar Bowl. In the
bowl, he was unable to get a passing game
going because the field was ankle-deep in
mud. But he sparked a 3-2 victory over
Louisiana State with another of his skills:
punting. "Sammy Baugh's steady barrage of
punting," a reporter wrote, "was the most
brilliant kicking exhibition ever seen in the
historic bowl."

By then Sammy was a Texas hero. His
teammates resented all the publicity he was
getting. They began razzing him. They called
him "The Great Baugh," and told him that,
in case he didn't know it, there were some

other players on the team too. Sammy couldn't understand why people were picking on him. He hadn't asked reporters to single him out in their stories. And he wasn't boasting about how good he was or asking for special favors. He didn't run around to parties where everyone could make a big fuss over him. In fact he didn't even *like* parties. He had a steady girl whom he'd been dating since high school, and he spent quiet evenings with her; otherwise he just studied and played football. He began to wonder if he should do so much passing during games. Maybe he ought to give the other fellows the ball more often. But after all he was only following his coach's instructions.

Meyer saw what was going on and called a team meeting — for everyone but Sammy. "Men," he said, "Sam is beginning to think you believe he's hogging the show. Now I believe the best way for us to win is for him to pass, so quit kidding him."

After this, the other players stopped harassing Sammy. Instead, with Sammy leading them, they spent the 1936 season harassing opponents. In the last game of the regular season they went West to play Santa Clara, the only unbeaten, untied team in the country. Santa Clara was the favorite, but

TCU had Baugh; his passing and punting
won the game 9–0. Then came the Cotton
Bowl and another spectacular show by
Sammy as TCU beat Marquette, the top
team in the Midwest, 16–6. None of the TCU
players ever kidded Sammy after that. They
all agreed that there had never been a passer
like him.

Other people agreed too — the All-America selectors, for instance. They put Sammy
on their teams. And a man named George
Preston Marshall wanted to put Sammy on
his team too. Marshall's team was the NFL
Redskins, who had played in Boston for five
years and were now about to play their first
season in Washington. Marshall hadn't been
able to attract many fans in Boston, and he
wasn't sure he'd attract them in Washington
either. But he'd have an awfully good
chance, he felt, if he could sign the hottest
passer in America, Sammy Baugh.

Marshall picked Sammy in the NFL draft,
but wasn't positive he could sign him. The
problem was baseball. Sammy still loved
baseball, and the St. Louis Cardinals had
offered him a contract.

Marshall spent weeks talking to Sammy
on the telephone and finally convinced him
to fly up to Washington for a meeting. There,

Marshall talked fast. "What can you lose, Sam?" he said. "Play for me this fall for the highest pay check a player ever got, plus a bonus for signing. Then, if you want, you can try baseball next spring. After that you can make up your mind."

Sammy went back to Texas, thought about it awhile, then called Marshall. "I'll sign," Sammy said.

"Great!" said Marshall. "Now listen, Sam. Before you come up here be sure to go out and buy a ten-gallon hat and some of those Texas boots. Get the best. I'll give you the money when you get here."

"Sure," said Sammy, "but what size?"

"What size? Don't you know what size you wear?"

"Of course I do," said Sammy. "I thought they were for you."

"No, no, no," Marshall said. "I want you to be wearing them when you step off the plane."

"I never wore such a getup in my life," Sammy said.

"Well, you'll be wearing them up here," Marshall said. "Up here you're a rootin', tootin' cowboy."

Marshall began to tell Washington fans that he was going to treat them to the most colorful star in sports. "Not only is he the best passer ever," Marshall said, "but he's a rootin', tootin' Texas cowboy as well." The combination was unbeatable, and crowds of people bought tickets.

Baugh didn't let Marshall down. Playing for the College All-Stars in the annual summer game against the defending NFL champions, Sammy threw a 47-yard touchdown pass in the first period. It was the only score of the game as the All-Stars beat the Green Bay Packers 6-0 — the first victory for the college boys in the series.

In his first NFL game Sammy completed eleven of sixteen passes against the New York Giants. The passes gained 116 yards and brought the Redskins a 13-3 win. Rolling along on Sammy's passing, the 'Skins won eight of eleven games and the Eastern Conference championship.

The title game was against the Bears in the biting cold and whipping wind of Chicago's Wrigley Field. But weather didn't stop Sammy. On the first play he faded back and flung the ball 43 yards to Cliff Battles. Moments later Battles scored the first touchdown on a seven-yard run. The Bears tied the game, then went ahead 14-7, but in the third period Sammy passed 55 yards to Wayne

Star passer of the Washington Redskins — "Slinging Sammy" Baugh. He retired in 1952 with eight NFL records. Fellow quarterback Sid Luckman once said of Sammy, "Nobody is ever going to equal him. Not anybody."

Milner and the score was 14-14. Chicago went
ahead again with another touchdown, but
Sammy wasn't about to let that go. With the
Redskins on their own 23, he roamed the
backfield and dodged around, waiting for
someone to get free. Finally he spotted Milner between defenders, cocked his arm, and
zoomed one of those bullet passes he used to
put through tires as a boy. The ball hit Milner's hands on the 48, and the Redskin end
sped untouched into the end zone.

Seven minutes later, with the score 21-21,
Sammy dropped back again. He searched the
horizon until he saw Charles Malone cutting
across. Then he pumped his arm, the ball
pointing right at Malone. But Sammy never
let go of the ball. Instead, while the Bears
rushed over to Malone, Sammy drew back
his arm again and threw to the other side,
to halfback Ed Justice. Nobody was near
Justice as he caught the ball and ran into the
end zone on the 35-yard play that won the
game 28-21.

Sammy had accomplished a lot. He had
put the Redskins in the championship game
and he had won it for them, completing 18
passes against the Bears for 335 yards and
three touchdowns. He had brought the fans
out to see the new Washington team, and he
was the biggest star in pro football.

But he still wanted to play baseball. When he left Washington at the end of the season, he let George Marshall know that if he made it with the Cardinals, he would probably not be back.

Through the early weeks of spring training, people in the Cardinal camp talked most about two rookie infielders: Sammy and a young shortstop named Marty Marion. They were both great, everyone agreed. It was hard to tell which was better. But then the big-league curve balls began coming up to the plate, and while Marion hit them with the finesse that one day would help make him a major-league all-star, Sammy kept striking out and popping up. The Cardinals sent him to their Columbus farm team, but he couldn't hit there either. Then he was shipped to the Rochester farm team and had the same problem. George Marshall was not exactly unhappy. He arranged a meeting with Baugh and said, "Sam, already you're the biggest thing in football and you've got ten years ahead of you. You haven't got five years in baseball. Sign here." Sammy signed and gave up baseball.

In '38 the Redskins finished second, and in '39 they faded further back — but only because some of their other stars were get-

ting old. Sammy was still sensational. In
1940, with some new talent supporting him,
Sammy set NFL records for most completed
passes (111), most touchdown passes (12),
and the longest touchdown pass (81 yards).
He also boomed out an 85-yard punt. The
'Skins won the division championship, then,
in the most disappointing game of Sammy's
career, were whomped by the Bears 73-0 in
the title playoff.

The next year Sammy completed 106 passes
as the Redskins slumped. In 1942 he completed 225 for 1,935 yards and 16 touchdowns — all records — and with a 48.7
average led the league in punting for the
third straight year.

That year Washington won the division
title. They came to the title game with a 10-1
record. But Washington's opponents, the
Bears, had an 11-0 record. The Bears had as
good a defense as any pro football team ever
put together, and their quarterback, Sid
Luckman, was the same one who had riddled
the Redskins 73-0 in 1940.

The Bears scored first and, after missing
the conversion, led 6-0. They kicked off and
got their pass defense set, and Sammy sent
all his receivers short. He floated back and
cocked his arm, and the Bears raced up to

cover. Then, with the Bears drawn in, Sammy
suddenly dropped his arm and boomed out a
quick kick. The ball flew up the field, hit the
ground, and kept rolling. It rolled all the
way to the Bear five.

In a hole, Luckman threw a pass and it
was intercepted. Now it was Baugh's turn.
Picking out Wilbur Moore amid the Bear
defensive backs, Sammy whipped the ball into
Moore's belly for a 25-yard touchdown. The
kick afterward was accurate, and those were
all the points Washington needed. The final
score was 14-6.

The Redskins and Bears met for the title
again in 1943. But early in the game Baugh
was carried off the field, suffering from a
concussion, and Chicago won. In 1944 the
Redskins abandoned the single-wing formation for the T, and they spent a season adjusting. But in 1945 Baugh completed an
astonishing .703 per cent of his passes as a
T-quarterback, and the Redskins won the
conference title, then lost to the Rams in the
playoff.

By then Sammy was thirty-one years old.
Off seasons he spent his time on a 6,000-acre
ranch in Abilene, Texas. Sammy probably
worked even harder there than he did on the
football field. He would rise with the sun and

put in a full day — fence riding, branding,
doctoring sick cattle, and farming. He loved
the work and he loved the solitude — his
ranch was tucked away at the foot of twin
peaks, sixteen miles from the nearest town.
He and his wife and their three children
rarely left the ranch, except to go into town
for a Saturday-afternoon movie, or to a rodeo when Sammy was competing.

Rodeo was Sammy's hobby, and his specialty was calf roping. "He throws a rope the
same way he throws a pass," a reporter observed. "He holds the loop close to his head,
and when he lets go, the lariat whistles past
his ear. More often than not, the rope reaches
its target, just as the football does. Baugh
has won money in numerous calf-roping contests and is accepted throughout the West
Texas rodeo circuit as a tough competitor."

But still, much as he loved the rodeo and
ranch life, Sammy kept coming back to play
football. After 1945 the Redskins never won
another title with Baugh, but he remained a
star for seven more seasons. In 1947 he completed 210 passes for 2,938 yards and 25
touchdowns. In 1948 he passed for 446 yards
in a single game. In 1949, his thirteenth
year in the NFL, he won the league's passing
championship for the sixth time. Baugh rolled

on until 1952; that year he completed the last
11 passes he would ever throw in pro football
— 11 passes in a row!

Sammy retired with eight NFL records:
among them, most passes completed, most
yards gained, most touchdown passes, and
highest passing percentage. He also retired
with as fine a compliment as any pro football
player ever had. It came from his number
one rival, the great quarterback Sid Luckman, who had led the Bears to five conference
and four league championships. "I like to
just sit and watch Sammy," Luckman said.
"Every time he throws, I learn something.
Nobody is ever going to equal him. Not anybody."

Record-Breaking Runner

IT was moments before the most important game of his life. Jimmy Brown and his Cleveland teammates were standing behind the end zone, waiting to be introduced to the huge crowd. The Cleveland Browns were playing the Baltimore Colts for the 1964 NFL championship, and the players were running onto the field, one by one, as the public-address announcer called their names. Suddenly Jimmy Brown had a terrible thought: "When I'm introduced, what if I run through the goalposts, slip, and fall flat on my face? What would people think?"

But when his name *was* called, Jimmy Brown ran through the goalposts with perfect balance, in a burst of speed. And when the game began, he ran through the Baltimore Colts the same way. Plunging into the middle of the line, he continually picked up important short gains. Running around end, he broke away once for 46 yards. And when he flared out from his fullback position to catch passes, he was always a threat. In all the years Jimmy had been with the Cleveland Browns they'd never won a world championship, and he wanted a victory more than ever before.

He got one this day. Cleveland had won 27-0. The Brown's quarterback, Frank Ryan, told him, "If you weren't human, I'd have given you the ball on every play."

Sometimes it seemed as if the Cleveland Browns actually did give the ball to Jimmy Brown on every play. He was with them from 1957 through 1965. In those nine years he carried the ball 2,359 times — more than anyone else in pro football history. He carried it with power, with speed, and with grace. He ran with his body high, his hips and shoulders swiveling. When he was hit he would fling out a forearm, swing a hip, dip his shoulder into the tackler, and keep driving.

Jimmy was six feet two inches tall and 228 pounds. He drove with so much impact that it usually took more than one man to bring him down. "When he comes through that line," linebacker Sam Huff once said, "brother, you just have to forget about yourself and dive in there to try and stop him.

You have to hit him from the knees down, or you don't have a prayer. Anything from the hips up, he'll either drag you with him or run right over you. Believe me, he's run over me more than once."

Jimmy's power was astounding, and so was his speed. Watching him crash the line, the tendency was to forget about his speed, to think of him as the kind of fullback who gets a couple of yards at a time by brute strength alone. But dozens of times in a season fullback Brown would crash into the opposing line, pop free, and turn on the speed. When he did that, when he raced away to the end zone, he looked like a champion sprinter in a track meet.

In his nine-year career Jimmy Brown set eleven National Football League records. He set a record for the most touchdowns ever scored in a career, 126. He set records for most yards gained by a runner in a career, 12,312; in a single season, 1,863; and in a single game, 237. He led the league in rushing for eight years — a record — five of them in a row, another record. And over his nine years he averaged 5.22 yards every time he carried the ball. No other player comes even close to that average.

Jimmy's contributions to his team went beyond his ball carrying. He set a standard

Jimmy Brown (No. 32) gains yardage as Gene Hickerson runs interference. When Brown retired in 1965, he had set a record for the most touchdowns ever scored in a career: 126.

of excellence for his teammates. After the
game in 1964, when the Browns won the
NFL championship, the Clevelands' coach
Blanton Collier made a special trip to Jimmy's locker. "Jim," Collier said, "I want to
thank you for your leadership."

Jimmy was not an easy man to know.
"Even if you lived next door to Jim," Myron
Cope once wrote, "you'd have difficulty know-
ing him thoroughly." When Cope paid a visit
to Dr. Clifton R. Hines, who lived next door
to Jimmy, Dr. Hines told him, "Jim minds
his own business. That's the type of fellow
he is. You'd never know he was a big ce-
lebrity. He's just a neighbor — we talk about
how to get the grass to grow better."

"Still," Cope wrote, "Dr. Hines has observed that Jim indulges himself almost to
excess in three departments: clothes, food,
and music. 'He has shoes on top of shoes,
hats on top of hats, and suits on top of suits,'
says Dr. Hines. . . . Incredulously, Dr.
Hines has watched Jim toss down a bowl of
fruit, a bowl of shrimp, several lobster tails,
a large steak, and a heaping dish of ice
cream with no damage to the flat 32-inch
waist. 'When he enters his house he wants
food and music,' says Dr. Hines. 'One of the
first things he does when he comes into the
house is turn on his record player.' "

Jimmy Brown wanted other things too. Those other things helped prompt his retirement from football in 1966. He was still only thirty years old then and could have had many more strong seasons in pro football. When he retired, he said he was going to pursue an acting career and also "take part in the struggle going on in my country" by working with an organization called the National Negro Industrial and Economic Union. "It's my brainchild," Brown said, "to help my fellow Negroes. We hope to provide financing for colored businessmen who find it difficult to obtain financing through normal channels. The real basis of the Negro's problem is economics. We think we can get Negroes to help themselves."

Jimmy knew about the problems Negroes faced in both the North and the South. He was born on St. Simon's Island, Georgia, in 1936. Soon afterward his parents split up, and his mother went to New York to work as a domestic, leaving Jimmy with his great-grandmother. Jimmy stayed in Georgia for seven years until his mother was able to send for him. Then he came to Manhasset, Long Island, where he attended grade school and then high school. In high school he starred in several sports and won thirteen letters in all. A scholarship took him to Syracuse Uni-

versity, and there he received varying All-
America ratings in football, basketball, and
lacrosse. As a football halfback in his senior
year, he scored 106 points in 1956 and set a
school rushing record of 986 yards. He scored
43 points (six touchdowns and seven conversions) in his final regular-season game
against Colgate, and then closed out his college career with 21 points (three touchdowns
and three conversions) against Texas Christian University in the Cotton Bowl. Jimmy
reported to the Browns in the summer of
1957. He had to beat out a veteran star, Ed
(Big Mo) Modzelewski, to get into the starting backfield.

Jimmy did not immediately impress people, Big Mo recalled years later. "We were
playing an exhibition against the Lions,"
said Big Mo, "and he'd just come in from the
All-Star game at Chicago. He didn't know
the plays very well and wasn't very sure of
himself. He didn't look too good, so I figured,
'Well, he's just another challenger.' There'd
been others. One kid before Jim — an All-
America from Colorado — was supposed to
be the greatest thing since penicillin. But
they cut him and he went back to selling en-
cyclopedias or something, and I kept playing
fullback. So my first reaction to Jim was just

that: probably another encyclopedia salesman.

"Then there was another thing going against him. The law of the jungle. Let's face it, I had a lot of friends on the team. They'd try to hit Jim just a little harder than they normally would hit in practice. But he'd bust out of their arms, and gradually you could see them gaining respect. You could see them thinking, 'Maybe he'll help us to a championship.' The writing was on the wall for me, so I became his number one rooter. You know, I doubt Jim ever knew the guys were hitting him extra hard."

Jim didn't know, but it didn't matter. He won the starting fullback job, gained 942 yards his rookie season, and scored 10 touchdowns. And he began to show traits that would one day help him become a leader of the Browns. Hal Lebowitz, Cleveland *Plain Dealer* sports editor, once described those traits as follows:

"Jim Brown is stoic and spartan. He doesn't drink water during the game. He has disciplined himself to show no emotion. Whether one man tackles him or he's dropped by a mob, he gets up slowly to conserve his energy for the next play. He never permits himself to reveal that he is in pain or that he is tired."

Around the league everyone knew that the rookie Jimmy Brown was going to be a special kind of star. He proved they were right. During the next three seasons he gained a total of 4,113 yards and scored 43 touchdowns. Many people thought that Paul Brown, who was then the Cleveland coach, relied on Jimmy too much. They were afraid that the young fullback's career would be cut short because of overwork. "Paul Brown is going to ruin Jimmy Brown," one of Jimmy's teammates said one day. "No man, not even a powerhouse like Jimmy, should carry the ball so much. The more he smashes into those big linemen, the more chance he has of getting hurt and ending his career. Sure, let him carry a lot, but at least give him a rest once in a while. He's not a horse; he's only a human being."

In a game against the Giants, Jimmy got hit in the head while carrying the ball in the first quarter. He was groggy and glassy-eyed the rest of the game; in fact he couldn't even remember the score. But still, after sitting out the second quarter, he played the third and fourth. The Browns lost 48-7, and afterward one of the Giants said, "It was a crime to send Jimmy back in after he got hurt. There was no point in it. We had the game wrapped up, and that guy was in a daze. He could have got hurt pretty badly."

Paul Brown argued back. "I'm not in the habit of asking Giant players what to do in a game," said the Cleveland coach. "But I do ask the team doctor."

Although there was no open friction at the time, Jimmy resented very much having been put back in the game. And over the next few years he became more and more angered at the way Paul Brown ran the club. Jimmy thought the coach was wrong in calling plays from the bench and in not giving the quarterback freedom to direct the team on the field. Jimmy didn't like the way the coach treated the players. He felt that Paul Brown considered them robots, not humans.

Jimmy had other gripes too, and so did many other Cleveland players. It all came to a head after the 1962 season, when a group of the Browns, including Jimmy, let the Cleveland owner, Art Modell, know they no longer wanted to play for Paul Brown.

Modell might have defended the coach if the Browns had been winning championships. But they hadn't won one since 1957, so he fired Paul Brown and replaced him with Blanton Collier. In 1963, Collier's first season as coach, Jimmy had his greatest season, setting a league record by gaining 1,863

yards. That year he also played one of his
five greatest games.

It was against the Giants on October 13,
in Yankee Stadium, New York. The Browns
came into the game unbeaten. But this one
was with the Eastern Conference defending
champions. Moments after the opening kickoff, New York's Dick Lynch intercepted a
pass and ran 48 yards for a touchdown. With
Jimmy ripping off large gains, the Browns
came back, moving 78 yards to the Giant one-
yard line. Then they gave the ball to Jimmy
once more, and he brought it in for the tying
touchdown.

Two more touchdowns were scored in the
first half, one by each team, but the Giants
also got a field goal. So New York was ahead
17-14 as the third period began. Then Jim
Brown took charge.

Three minutes after the second-half kickoff, Jimmy swung wide, caught a screen pass,
and zigzagged 72 yards for a touchdown. A
few minutes after that he took a handoff in
the backfield, raced to his left, suddenly reversed his field, and ran to his right. Legs
churning   smoothly,   shoulders   dipping
slightly, head up, he seemed to be gliding
as he turned the end and sped 32 yards for
another touchdown. The Browns had all the
points they needed for a victory.

Nevertheless the Browns didn't win the '63 championship. Slumping late in the season, they finished with a 10-4 record, second in the East to the Giants, who were 11-3. The next year, though, was 1964. The Browns won the NFL title, then came back the following year to win the Eastern Conference title. The last game Jimmy Brown played in pro football was the '65 title playoff, the Browns against the Green Bay Packers. It was a sad farewell, Cleveland losing 23-12 and Jimmy not playing particularly well.

Certainly Jimmy Brown would have loved to have made his final game a memorable one, but really he had won his place in pro football history long before that. Ed Modzelewski talked about that place one day. Big Mo was the man who lost his job to Jimmy and then stayed on for a few seasons as Jimmy Brown's substitute. "I'll tell you," Big Mo said, "I feel like the guy who played behind Babe Ruth."

Whip-Cracking Coach

THE Green Bay Packers knew one thing for sure as they filed into their 1959 training camp. They knew that this season was going to be different from last. In 1958 they had been the worst team in professional football, losing ten games and winning only one. Now they had a new head coach, a man named Vince Lombardi, and they were certain he'd be making changes. They didn't know too much else about him — only that he'd been a great guard in college some decades ago, and more recently had been an assistant coach for the United States Military Academy and the New York Giants.

The Packers' previous coach hadn't been a particularly tough man, and they wondered if Lombardi would be tough. Six months earlier, when he'd taken the Packer job, Lombardi had told the club's board of directors, "I want it understood that I'm in complete command here." What kind of command would that be?

The players found out fast. The first day of training was an exhausting one, full of calisthenics and muscle-aching running, and the morning of the second day twenty Packers swarmed the trainer's room and waited to be treated for minor injuries. Suddenly the new coach appeared. "What's this?" he boomed, and his voice seemed to shake the ceiling. "You've got to play with those small hurts, you know!" The day after that only two players showed up in the trainer's room, and one of them, a big end with a swollen ankle, had his feet in a bucket of ice when the coach showed up. "How you feeling?" the coach asked, and again that big voice rose to the rafters. The end hopped out of his chair and began to rush out of the room. "I feel better already, Coach," he said.

So the Packers found out about their new coach: he was tough. Vince Lombardi was very tough. From that very first day in 1959, until he retired as coach in 1968, he remained very tough. His five Western Conference titles, his four National Football League championships, his two Super Bowl victories — all of them were the result of his dedication to discipline and detail.

"Coach treats us all the same — just like

dogs," Green Bay's defensive tackle Henry
Jordan once said. And indeed it often seemed
that way. Year in, year out, the players complained a lot about the discipline, particularly in the summer training camp. There he
whipped them into shape by running them
ragged, by forcing them to exert themselves
until their breath was gone and their muscles
were sore. The team griped about Vince's
methods. It was a system so tough that players were fined five hundred dollars — $500!
— for breaking curfew or for being caught
merely standing — not drinking — at an
off-limits bar. The players resented this but
feared him. They were nervous even when
breaking the smallest rules.

But somehow, every year, as loud and
strong as they always were in the summer,
the complaints dwindled down as the season
progressed. By January, when that championship was clinched and those bonus checks
were coming in, every Packer was admitting
Vince Lombardi's system brought victories.

It was a system that demanded even more
from the coach than from the players. The
players had to abide by the system, but the
coach had to create it. And Lombardi began
creating it the moment he took the job in
January, 1959. He signed on as general manager as well as coach, so that he could have

complete control over hiring and firing and trading and scouting. Immediately he hired four of the best assistant coaches he could find. One of them was Phil Bengtson, the man who in 1968 would replace Vince as head coach. Then Lombardi more than doubled the scouting staff. He built it to over sixty part-time and full-time scouts; then he put in a system of cross-checking, so that each prominent college star would be inspected a minimum of twenty times by at least ten different men. Following that, Lombardi sat down with his assistant coaches, and for months they ran and reran films of all the Packers' 1958 games.

Looking at the films, Lombardi saw that there were certain players who did not have the skills or hustle to fit into the kind of offense and defense he wanted to use. He made mental notes to have them released or traded. He saw others who were playing positions they weren't suited for, but who did have raw talent. He made up his mind to try them at new positions. The basic game he wanted his squad to play was one that relied on teamwork and precision, each singular mission part of a total pattern, every man on the field moving at the same time in a particular order. One of his most familiar war cries through the years was a demand for the

players to move as a unit. "All together!" he
would bellow. "Get off all together! Not like
a typewriter!"

He wanted speed on his defensive unit. He
wanted that defense moving fast and gliding
in chorus. He knew exactly the kind of men
who could make such a defense work, and he
made trades for players like Jordan and Wil-
lie Davis, two defensive linemen who were
second-stringers at Cleveland but became
All-Pros at Green Bay. For his offense he
wanted fast linemen too, particularly at the
guards, because he was ready to install a
play that one day would become the heart of
the Packers' success: the power sweep. On
the power sweep, the ball carrier would circle
the end and both guards would have to get
out in front of him to block. Since one of the
guards would have to get there from the far
side of the center, he would have to be quick.
Lombardi decided that the Packers had one
guard who qualified for that role — a
youngster named Jerry Kramer. But he
needed another, because the power sweep
would sometimes be run to the right side and
sometimes to the left. Checking around, he
picked up a veteran named Fuzzy Thurston,
who'd been a failure with four pro teams.

But Lombardi would also have to keep
many of the players, even though the Packers

had been the worst team in pro football in 1958. He decided that a second-string full-back, Jim Taylor, could be his first-string fullback, and that a substitute quarterback, Bart Starr, might eventually be his first-string quarterback. Lombardi was convinced that a fellow who'd alternated as a quarter-back and fullback in the past was the man he wanted at halfback, the key position in his planned offense. That man was Paul Hor-nung.

As an assistant coach with the Giants, Lombardi had designed a special play — the option pass — for Frank Gifford, and it had been one of the critical weapons in the New York attack. On that play Gifford would swing around end and have two choices: to throw a pass or continue running. Now Vince wanted to use that play with Hornung. "The option of course is taken off the end run sweep," Hornung has explained. "The block-ing is the same as the end run sweep, and the object is that it's supposed to look like the sweep. The reason the option is there is that if all the potential receivers are covered, then it does become an end sweep. The tight end blocks the linebacker for three counts, just as he does on end sweeps, and the only difference is that he releases. And the flanker is already downfield as he is in the end sweep,

and you have your guards pulling, and the
fullback is blocking the end the same way as
the end sweep. So if everybody is covered
you just holler — go! — you know. And if
they're not covered, naturally you're just
going to throw a pass."

The option pass was about the only frill
in Lombardi's offense. Otherwise it was a
basic ball-control system. It was built upon
power running to grind out the yards and
enough passes, particularly surprise long
passes, to keep the defense off-balance. The
main thing in Vince's offense, as well as his
defense, was that everybody had to work
together and everybody had to work hard,
had to do something, on every play.

The Packers put Vince's system to work,
and the team that had won only a single
game in 1958 won seven and lost five in
1959. The year after that they won the Western Conference title. They lost the championship playoff to the Philadelphia Eagles, but
in 1961 they won the world championship,
walloping the Giants 37-0 in the playoff.
Vince Lombardi was acknowledged as the
top coach in pro football and many of the
players he had steered along — men like
Hornung and Davis and Thurston and tight
end Ron Kramer — were rated the best in
pro football at their positions.

In 1962 the Packers were world champions again. By then more of Lombardi's men — fellows like Jordan, middle linebacker Ray Nitschke, defensive back Herb Adderley, and offensive tackle Forrest Gregg — were showing up on the All-Pro lists. Lombardi, meanwhile, was driving his players, and himself as well, as hard as ever. His work routine hadn't softened with success. The week of a game he still spent Monday, an offday for the players, reporting to his office at nine a.m. to watch the films of Sunday's game and grade the performance of each Packer. Then, after the grading, he and his assistant coaches began shaping strategy for the next game, working until midnight, with only a couple of hours off for meals. Tuesday he held a light workout for the players, and afterward worked into the night with his assistants again. Wednesday he handed out offensive and defensive assignments to the players, then ran them through the plays they'd use for the upcoming game. After that he watched films with the players. Thursday and Friday were filled with more workouts and planning. Then, after trying to relax on Saturday — perhaps playing a round of golf — he was ready to coach and suffer through the Sunday game. Sometimes Vince actually seemed to be pushing himself

even harder than he had when he first came
to Green Bay. "It's hard to keep winning,"
he explained. "No other sport requires the
self-denial or dedication to continue winning
that football does."

The concept of working hard and of pushing himself and others with rigid discipline
dominated Vince long before he came to the
Packers. After a boyhood in Brooklyn, he
went to Fordham University and was part
of the toughest football team that school ever
assembled. It was probably one of the toughest ever to play college football. The linemen
on that team were nicknamed "The Seven
Blocks of Granite," and Vince was one of
the Blocks, a rough, hard-hitting guard.
Later he became a teacher and sports coach
at St. Cecilia's High School in Englewood,
New Jersey; and Father Timmy Moore, who
was the school's athletic director, once recalled that "Vince was as uncompromising in
the classroom as he was on the football field."
Vince taught chemistry, physics, and Latin
at St. Cecilia's. One day one of his girl students came into Father Tim's office crying.
She hadn't done her chemistry homework,
she told Father Tim, and she was afraid to
go to class. "There was nothing I could do for
her," Father Tim said, "and she knew she
was in for it because she had let Vince

down. Nobody let him down and got away
with it."

Once Vince cut an outstanding football
prospect from the St. Cecilia's squad because
the boy was caught smoking — something
the players were ordered not to do. "We
make a rule, we keep it," Vince said, sending
the boy home.

At St. Cecilia's, Vince's team won six state
championships in eight seasons. In one
stretch they went unbeaten in 36 straight
games. Vince went on to coach the Fordham
freshman team and assist in the coaching of
the varsity. Then he moved to the United
States Military Academy to work as an assistant to the Army head coach, Earl Blaik;
and after that, in his last stop before Green
Bay, he became offense coach for the Giants.
At the end of the '62 season, with the Packers
the world champions for the second year in a
row, Vince could look back upon association
with only two losing teams in twenty-four
years — one at Fordham in 1948, the other
at Army in 1951.

In '63 he had another winning team, di-
recting the Packers to eleven victories, two
losses, and one tie. But the Chicago Bears,
with eleven victories, one loss, and two ties,
won the Western Conference title. The next
year Green Bay was second to Baltimore in

UPI

Green Bay players, led by tackle Forrest Gregg (No. 75),
crowd in to congratulate coach Vince Lombardi as the
Packers beat the Los Angeles Rams to clinch the 1965
NFL Western Conference title.

the Western Conference. In 1965 the Packers won the NFL title again, defeating Cleveland 23-12 in the playoff. In 1966 the Packers not only won the NFL championship but the first Super Bowl game as well, clobbering the AFL champs, the Kansas City Chiefs, 35-10.

At the beginning of the 1967 season, however, people said that the Packer dynasty had ended. Their reasoning made sense. Hornung was gone, picked up by the New Orleans Saints in the 1967 expansion draft. Taylor had insisted upon being traded to New Orleans too. Jim Ringo, the All-Pro center of the early years, and Ron Kramer, the tight end, had both been gone for a couple of seasons. Many of the old stars who remained, including Thurston and the flashy split end, Max McGee, had slowed down.

Vince had been getting replacements ready of course. He had some fine young ballplayers, particularly a pair of spectacular running backs, Jim Grabowski and Donny Anderson. But most people felt that the youngsters weren't yet of championship caliber.

Early in the '67 season the skeptics seemed right. The Packers lost a few ball games, and even when they won they were hardly overpowering. Then, on top of that, injuries set

in. Grabowski, who had replaced Taylor as
starting fullback, got hurt. Elijah Pitts, the
number one halfback, went out for the season with an injury. But playing with backs
like Ben Wilson, a castoff from the Los Angeles Rams, and Chuck Mercein, a castoff from
the New York Giants, Lombardi somehow
managed to whip his team to important victories. "Torn and bleeding at the midpoint,"
Jerry Izenberg wrote, "the Packers were
running flat out at the finish when they won
the games they had to win."

In 1967 the NFL had broken the Western
Conference into two divisions — the Coastal
and the Central — and the Eastern Conference into two — the Century and the Capi-
tol. Under the new alignment, the Coastal
and Central champions had to meet at the
end of the season for the Western title. The
Packers won the Central championship, and
the Los Angeles Rams won the Coastal. The
Rams came into the Green Bay game easily
the hottest team in pro football. Searching
for something extra, something to give his
Packers an added push, Vince delivered a
rousing speech in the locker room before the
game. "This," he said, "is the most important
game of your life."

The Packers beat the Rams, then came up
against the Eastern Conference champions,

the Dallas Cowboys. Again Vince delivered a stirring pep talk. *"This,"* he said, "is the most important game of your life."

Once more the Packers responded with a victory, and a few days later Doug Hart, a reserve defensive back, said, "For two straight games he's told me it's the most important game of my life, and the heck of it is that for two straight games he's been right and I know it."

A final game remained: the Super Bowl — Green Bay against the Oakland Raiders. Only Vince knew it, but the Super Bowl would be his last game as the Packer coach. Other people suspected he might retire and concentrate only on being the general manager, but he kept saying he hadn't yet made up his mind. Inside, though, he knew.

The Super Bowl wasn't the toughest game the Packers played in the '67 season, and it wasn't the best game they played. But it was an appropriate one for Vince to retire on, because it was the game in which the Packers best mirrored the teachings of the coach. With precision and teamwork, the Packers won simply by grinding down the Raiders. There was no key moment, no dramatic innovation. The Raiders simply never knew what happened. The Packers picked at them and pried at them and controlled the ball. A

field goal here, a touchdown there, another
field goal. Methodically, almost covertly, they
put points on the scoreboard, and suddenly
the Raiders looked up and they were out of
the ball game.

Then Vince Lombardi announced his retirement. And Jerry Kramer, who had been
with Vince from that first year in Green
Bay, tried to explain how the coach had piled
up that incredible record. "He stands up in
the locker room," said Kramer, "and he says
that football players are a dime a dozen, and
you nod your head up and down and all the
while you are saying, 'Bull, bull, bull.' Then
he says, 'Men with more talent than you have
sat in this room, but they're not here now,'
and you nod again and say, 'Bull, bull, bull.'
And then he says, 'You're here because you
make this team what it is. You're here because all of you *fit*.' And then one day you
stop nodding — because you know that's the
way it really is."

"Nobody Tackles Jim"

YEAR in, year out, whenever people came up to him to talk about sports, they would end up by asking, "What was the best day you ever had, Jim?" He would shake his head, shrug his broad shoulders, and reply, "Don't know about that. I was in a lot of games in a lot of places."

He certainly was. Pro football games and college football games, major-league baseball games, and Olympic Games. He was Jim Thorpe, and he was the greatest athlete ever.

In 1950 the *Associated Press* asked 393 sportswriters to vote on the outstanding athlete of the half-century. Thorpe won with 252 first-place votes. But even long before the poll was taken, everyone knew what a great athlete Jim Thorpe was. They knew it back in 1912. That year Jim was already established as a football star, and he turned to track and field. He swept through the five

105

In 1950, sportswriters voted Jim Thorpe the outstanding athlete of the half-century. He played baseball, won Olympic championships, and starred in college and pro football.

pentathlon events and the ten decathlon events at the Olympic Games in Stockholm to win a pair of gold medals. After that performance, Sweden's King Gustav V said to Thorpe, in wonder, "You, sir, are the greatest athlete in the world."

Thorpe's reply was as simple and informal as he was. He answered, amid all that royal pomp and splendor, "Thanks, King."

There were few frills to Jim Thorpe. He was tough, rough-hewn, down to earth. When he ate, he ate a lot; when he ran, he ran flat out; and when he smacked a baseball, he went for the long ball. Of course, when he ran with a football, he faked with his head and jiggled his hips. He is remembered most, though, for the way he tucked that football under his arm and simply ran over people. He is remembered for the way he tackled — jarring contests, one man's strength against another's. And how he punted — long, booming spirals that were propelled into the air by pure power. In these days, when nobody dropkicks any more, he is also remembered for the way he made field goals, with no aid from a holder — he simply dropped the ball to the ground himself. Then, as it hit, he would thrust those strong toes into it and orbit it as many as 50 yards and over the goalposts.

Jim was born on Oklahoma farmland in 1888, a member of the Sac and Fox Indian tribe. As a boy he helped raise hogs, cattle, and horses, and he ran in the woods with his two brothers. He tracked game, hunted deer, fished. At ten he bagged his first deer. At fifteen he could rope and ride a wild pony and was an excellent shot with a rifle. He attended grade school on the Sac and Fox reservation and was one of the few Indians in the nation at that time who were lucky enough to go on in school after elementary school.

He enrolled at the Carlisle Indian School in Pennsylvania. "Carlisle was a prep school rather than a college," one writer, Frank Graham, Jr., has noted, "but though its classes only went to the twelfth grade, many of its students were in their twenties.

"Although the school had over a thousand students, most of them were too young or too old to play college football. Nevertheless the few young men considered eligible for football were almost all of exceptional athletic ability. Carlisle, of necessity, played a major-college schedule; small schools wouldn't play them because they were too tough."

Jim was nineteen when he tried out for the varsity; he was a lean, strong six-footer. One day during practice the coach, Pop Warner,

was urging the team to get mean, and repri-
manding the players for poor tackling. "Let's
have some tackling practice now," he bel-
lowed, and motioned for the starting eleven
to punt.

The punt went into the air. Thorpe caught
it and ran through everybody. On the next
punt he charged straight ahead, passed two
tacklers, knocked over four more, and was in
the end zone again. "No, no!" an assistant
coach screamed at the starters. "Tackle!
Tackle!"

Thorpe looked up and said, "Nobody tackles Jim."

Jim made the team, but sat on the bench
through the first few games. Finally he got
his chance when Albert Payne, the number
one left halfback, was injured against Penn.
On his first play, Jim ran 65 yards for a
touchdown. The next time he got the ball he
ran 85 yards for a touchdown. "He was raw,"
an observer said, "unrehearsed in such things
as faking and using the sideline to advan-
tage, yet the big-time Penns looked like men
tied in knots."

That was the beginning. The next year,
1908, he kicked three field goals to beat
Penn State 12-5, then ran 60 yards for a
touchdown to tie Penn 6-6. He was out of
school in 1909 and 1910, but came back in

1911, scored 17 points in seventeen minutes against Dickinson, scored three touchdowns against Mount St. Mary's, and was spectacular in Carlisle's upsets of Pitt, Penn, and Lafayette. Then, against the defending national champions, Harvard, he kicked four field goals. The little Indian school won 18-15. In every game, opponents tried to beat Thorpe so hard he'd have to return to the bench; but the rougher they played, the rougher *he* played. During his college career a writer asked him if he'd ever been hurt, and Jim smiled and said, "Hurt? How could anybody get hurt playing football?"

In 1912 Colonel Joe Thompson, the Pitt coach, angered at his loss to Carlisle the previous season, said, "Thorpe will never run through us again. We've got him figured." When Thompson's words were relayed to him, Thorpe merely said, "Huh!" In the rematch with Pitt, Jim scored 32 points to spark a 45-8 victory.

The big game that year was against Army. The Army team ranked number two in the nation. As usual, Carlisle was the underdog, but the Indians scored first when Jim cracked the middle of the Army line for a touchdown. A minute later he threw a pass for a second touchdown, and still later he fielded a punt near his own 10-yard line, started wide, cut back, and ran straight up the field for a third touchdown. But the third touchdown was called back because of a penalty, and Army punted again. This time Thorpe picked up the ball on his five-yard line and ran 95 yards into the Army end zone. The final score was 27-6. Jim had scored 22 points and had played brilliantly on defense, and Carlisle had held Army to only four first downs. Jim led the nation in scoring that season with 198 points and 25 touchdowns.

Thorpe was active in track and field too, and Carlisle became known for its strength in the sport. But the publicity that accompanied the Carlisle track victories was often incomplete. Few people really knew exactly how the Indian school did it. Seeking to find out, and eager to see this powerful team close up, a crowd of Lafayette College students came to greet the train from Carlisle on the day of a Carlisle-Lafayette meet. The students were certain something had gone wrong when the train arrived and only two young men, Jim and a small fellow, jumped off.

"Where's the team?" one of the Lafayette students said.

"This is the team," Jim said.

"You mean just the two of you?"

"Nope," said Jim. "Just me. This little guy is the manager."

Jim took on the entire Lafayette squad and won eight first places.

There was no event Jim couldn't master. At one meet he saw some athletes flinging a heavy iron ball with a handle, and he asked, "What's that?"

"A hammer," someone said.

Jim stood by and watched them aim for a mark 140 feet away. None of them made it. He asked for a turn, imitated their motion, and threw it 145 feet.

Thorpe was so confident of his skills, he never felt he had to practice hard. On the ship to Sweden for the 1912 Olympics, he lay in his bunk while others worked out. In Sweden, waiting for the Games to begin, he took long naps in a hammock while athletes ran and jumped out on the field. Once he heard someone mention the distance his leading opponents were expected to leap in the broad jump. Jim leaped out of the hammock, measured off the distance, and looked at it closely. Certain he could jump that far, he climbed back in the hammock and continued his nap.

In the Olympics, he did everything. Winning the pentathlon gold medal, he was first in four of the five events — broad jump, discus throw, 200-meter, and 100-meter runs — missing out only in the javelin. Winning the ten-event decathlon, the toughest test of athletic skill anywhere, he placed first in the shot put, high hurdles, high jump, and 1,500 meters. He finished no lower than fourth in the six remaining events — pole vault, javelin, broad jump, discus, 400-meter, and 100-meter runs — and easily had the highest composite score. When he returned home there was a parade through the streets of New York in his honor, and he received the personal congratulations of the President of the United States, William Howard Taft.

After his heroic Olympic and football feats in 1912, Jim turned to baseball in 1913. He joined the New York Giants and played in the major leagues seven seasons, doing adequately enough but never approximating his success in football or track. In later years, when he was asked about his baseball career, he didn't talk much about his accomplishments on the field. He preferred to talk about other experiences as a baseball player, particularly those that involved the Giant manager, John McGraw. "We were shagging flies in the outfield before a game," Thorpe once said, "and Jeff Tesreau, who was a pretty good pitcher, began scuffling around with me. Finally I pinned him with an arm lock. The

next day McGraw wanted him to pitch, and
Jeff said he couldn't because he had a sore
arm. McGraw asked him what gave him a
sore arm, but Jeff wouldn't squawk, so Mc-
Graw said, 'You don't have to tell me. I saw
you wrestling with that big Indian yesterday. I'll have no more of that on this ball
club.' He called me in and threatened to fine
me if I roughhoused any of the other players, and I said that was all right with me
because I didn't want to roughhouse with
them anyway, but they were always chal-
lenging me.

"After that some of the other players used
to kid me. They'd tweak my nose or pull my
ears and dare me to tussle with them, and
I'd just laugh. But one guy got real nasty. He
kept calling me names, and I knew he wasn't
fooling. I warned him that I could take just
so much, but he kept on, and one day over
in Brooklyn I slapped him across the face.
He went crying to McGraw, and McGraw was
going to fine me, but I told him what happened. That night he released this guy to
the minors, and the guy never came back."

Following his third season of baseball,
Jim decided he'd like to try some pro football too. There was no National Football
League then — no pro football league at all
— but there were some teams playing the

game for money — teams like the Canton
Bulldogs and the Portsmouth Spartans and
the Rock Island Independents. Jim joined up
with Canton.

By then Jim no longer had his Olympic
gold medals. The Amateur Athletic Union
had discovered that back in 1909 Jim had
received some money for playing semipro
baseball, and they said he therefore had not
been an amateur in the Olympics. The AAU
ruled that his accomplishments could no
longer be listed in the official Olympic record
books and ordered him to return his medals.
But sports fans considered the AAU ruling
ridiculous. In their minds Jim Thorpe was
still the great Olympic champion, and they
loved him as much as ever. They came out to
see him play pro football — not in huge
crowds, but in bigger crowds than ever came
before. "Thorpe's drawing power," Tex
Maule writes in his official NFL history, "ani-
mated pro football from the time he joined
the Bulldogs in 1915 until 1925, when a new
star [Red Grange] arrived to project the
game onto another plateau of public accep-
tance."

Jim was as good in pro football as he'd
been in college. He was injured once in a
game against the Massillon Tigers, and Canton only managed a tie. The next week the

same teams met, and Thorpe was healthy. He scored 23 points, and nobody on either team scored another. In another Massillon-Canton game the Massillon end, Knute Rockne, determined to stop Thorpe. The first two times Thorpe ran around Rockne's end, Knute smashed him for losses. Looking up the second time, Thorpe said, "You shouldn't do that to Jim. Look at all those people who paid to see old Jim run."

"Well, go ahead and run — if you can," Rockne snapped.

On the next play, as Rockne used to tell the story, Jim swung wide and let him have it — knees, elbow, stiff-arm. He stomped over Rockne's body, raced 60 yards for a touchdown, and turned around to see Rockne being helped to his feet. "Nice work, Rock!" Jim shouted. "You sure let old Jim run."

Pro football was disorganized in those days, and there weren't many good referees. Play from whistle to whistle was like a street brawl. Jim brawled with the best. He wore special shoulder pads made of tough, hard leather, and "they hit like iron," recalls George Halas, who played against him. "He blocked with his shoulder, and it felt like he had hit you with a four-by-four. He was a great defensive player, too. If he hit you from behind, he'd throw that big body across your back and about break you in two."

Another pro football player of that era, Pete Calac, once said, "Jim had one way of running I never saw before. Not everyone wore helmets in those days, and Jim would shift his hip toward the guy about to tackle him, then swing it away and then, when the player moved in to hit him, he'd swing his hip back, hard, against the tackler's head and leave him lying there. He talked a lot during a game, too. I mean he'd say to a tackle on the other side, 'I'm coming right over'; then, like as not, he would."

Thorpe was with the Bulldogs in 1920 when representatives from eight of the teams got together to form an organized league. They called it the American Professional Football Association, and they elected Jim president. He served in that office for a year and also continued playing. The next year he stepped down and the league picked a new president, and the year after that — 1922 — the league picked a new name: the National Football League.

Jim played in the NFL until 1929, when he was forty-one. He slowed down as he got older, of course, but he still had bursts of brilliance. "Deep in his thirties," Al Stump

once wrote, "in one game of pro football at
Dayton, he put six men out of the game with
his brutal blocking." And Jimmy Conzelman
always liked to talk about the time "when
Thorpe was thirty-nine and I was playing
safety against him, and he punted over my
head, 75 yards on the fly."

When Jim retired from pro football, his
life as an athlete was at an end. He hit upon
hard times. He had trouble getting work that
he enjoyed. He was sick a lot of the time.
People cheated him out of much of his money.
The ones who had idolized him still talked
about him, but they didn't think about how
Jim might be making out. Once in a while
sad stories about him would get into the
newspapers — about how he was digging
ditches for a living, or how he couldn't afford
to buy a ticket for the 1936 Olympics in Los
Angeles — and then everyone would get interested in him and a few people would try
to help out. But after a while people would
forget. Jim Thorpe, the greatest athlete
ever, died penniless — without ever really
getting all the help he deserved and needed.

"Oh, No, Say It's Not You"

TO play pro football, Deacon Jones was saying, a man has to expect to suffer. And not only on the field. "I'm a big guy," he said. As if it needed proving, he stretched tall, towering above his listeners like a tree, and the muscles ballooned on his six-foot, five-inch, 260-pound body. "A big guy like me, I could eat a horse. I could eat so much I could easily weigh 290, 300 pounds or more. But at that size I'd lose my speed. So I've got to watch my diet. My wife puts a little bitty food in front of me and I say, 'Hey, what's this? Who you feeding, a midget?' She says, 'That's it, Jones. Eat it and make it last.' So that's what I do."

Deacon smiled. He had just come off the field after helping the Los Angeles Rams to a tough victory, and he was happy. But he was also sore all over. He had played a hard game at defensive end, battling players as big and bigger than he. "You've really got to suffer to last in this game," he said. "Sometimes I hurt so bad in games, I get tears in my eyes. The fans don't understand that. They think big guys like us don't hurt. We do. We bleed and we hurt. I wear so much tape people say I look like a mummy. The trainer puts ten, fifteen yards of tape on some of us, and still we get hurt. It's a very rough game out there. We call the inside of the line 'the pit.' That's a very good name for it. It's like a bunch of animals kicking and clawing and scratching at each other."

Few players have ever hit as hard as David (Deacon) Jones. And probably no big lineman was ever as fast as he. The combination of strength and speed helped to make him, in 1967, the most feared defensive player in football. Deacon suffered all right, but other men on other teams suffered more because *they* had to play against him. In one game some years back, Deacon knocked down the Green Bay quarterback, Bart Starr, four times. "He got in on me so quick," Starr said, "I thought he was one of my own backs." Deacon was really pleased when he heard what Starr had said. "Yes," said Deacon, "it was my greatest of many great games."

In another game, Cleveland's quarterback Frank Ryan rolled out to the opposite side of the field to avoid Jones. But when Ryan

Sport Magazine

Lineman Deacon Jones (No. 75) leaps high to block a pass thrown by Green Bay's Bart Starr. In 1967, Jones placed second in the NFL's Most-Valuable-Player poll — a rare honor for a defensive lineman.

looked up, there was Jones about to tackle him. "Please," said Ryan, "admit you were hiding out there waiting for me all the time!"

In still another game, Deacon stampeded from 20 yards behind to haul down Pittsburgh's speedy, 195-pound Marv Woodson. "Oh no," said Woodson, "say it's not you!"

"It's me," said Deacon. "It's me."

Quarterbacks, running backs, and pass receivers are usually the most celebrated players in football. The reason is that people generally follow a football game by following the ball, and these are the players who throw the ball, run with the ball, and catch the ball. But in 1967 defensive lineman Jones was so spectacular, he finished second in a poll taken by the Associated Press to pick the NFL's Most Valuable Player. It was a distant second, and far behind the winner, Baltimore quarterback Johnny Unitas, but still Deacon was delighted. "How about me being number two!" Deacon said. "I never even considered I'd get a vote, because they just don't vote for defensive linemen. I guess it's a good thing I didn't win it, or I'd be in a trance for a week."

"Now don't get so high," his teammate Roger Brown said. "You're not number one.

You're number two. You've got to try harder. You'll get your shot at number one on Sunday."

Deacon smiled. On Sunday the Rams would play the Baltimore Colts in their most important game of the season. The Colts were in first place in the NFL's Coastal Division, the Rams in second place. On Sunday, December 17, they would meet for the championship. The losing team would be all through for the season. The winner would go on into the postseason playoffs — the games that match up the division champions — and have a chance to play in the Super Bowl. "Maybe after Sunday," Deacon said to Roger Brown, "I'll demand a recount."

Deacon was expected to be one of the key men in the game. To win, the Rams would have to stop Unitas, and the biggest burden would be on their defensive linemen: Jones, Brown, Merlin Olsen, and Lamar Lundy. Nicknamed "The Fearsome Foursome," because they were so tough and talented at bursting through opponents' lines, they were being counted on to charge in and tackle Unitas before he could pass — or at least bother him enough to spoil his aim. If they were unable to rush in quickly, if Unitas had time to stand back and pick out his receivers, certainly he would riddle the Rams as he'd been riddling pro football teams for ten years.

Early in the game, The Fearsome Foursome couldn't break through. As a result, Unitas threw a touchdown pass to put the Colts ahead. At the sidelines the Rams' coach, George Allen, quickly cornered his defensive linemen. "You're going to have to rush harder, you linemen," Allen snapped. Deacon scowled, gulped water from a paper cup, and spit it to the ground.

Deacon and the others began bursting through. Time after time they swarmed Unitas, occasionally dumping him, often forcing him to throw while off-balance. Late in the first half, with the Rams leading 10-7, the Colts had the ball on the Los Angeles 27-yard line. Unitas backpedaled, looking for an open receiver. As Unitas faded back, Deacon crashed into the line, his big arms waving, his hands shoving at Colts, his feet driving.

Suddenly Deacon was free and diving for Unitas. Deacon was coming in at a wide angle and couldn't hit him solidly, but he managed to grab the quarterback's leg. He hung on, trying to twist Unitas to the ground, thinking, "I've gotta bring him down like you bulldog a steer." Careening, Unitas spotted a Colt downfield and began to throw. Suddenly, as Unitas released the ball and Deacon twisted, Olsen crashed the quarterback's arm. The ball wobbled short of the Colt, a Ram intercepted it, and the Rams went on to score a touchdown.

It was the key play of the game. After that the Rams had more than a large lead; they gained the momentum also. All through the second half, Jones and the rest of the Foursome blasted Unitas so often and so hard that the Colts couldn't get another touchdown. The Rams won 34–10.

In the playoffs the next week the Rams were beaten by the Green Bay Packers, who went on to win the championship of all of pro football. But still, 1967 had been a spectacular year for the Rams. In the eight seasons preceding it they had never finished higher than third in their division; three times they had finished last, and three times they were next to last. Looking back after the 1967 season, Deacon knew that the Rams had come a long way since he had joined them in 1961.

He came to the Rams by a long, hard route. David Jones was born in Eatonville, Florida, in 1938 and grew up in nearby Orlando. His father worked hard at the jobs available to Negroes in Orlando, earning wages as a gardener, carpenter, and general handyman, but there was rarely enough money in the house to comfortably feed and clothe eight children. "It was real tough for us," Deacon once said. "We did not have very much, and we did not have much to look forward to. Certainly there wasn't much opportunity."

Through high school Deacon helped out by working as a waiter, busboy, bellboy, short-order cook, chauffeur, and handyman. He also found time to star as a two-way tackle and end on the high school football team and to win letters in track, basketball, and baseball. His parents kept telling him it was important to get a college education, and Deacon listened. He enrolled first at Mississippi Vocational, then transferred to South Carolina State College in Orangeburg.

He was a versatile football star at those schools. "I even place-kicked," he once said. "I kicked a 48-yard field goal in college once. I not only played defense, but I caught passes and ran beautifully with them. I ran 75 yards with a pass to score against Florida State. I was a big star."

Still, since he played in the obscurity of small-college competition, few pro scouts noticed him. The Rams became aware of him by accident. While two of their scouts were studying films of a back on another team, they kept seeing a big fellow, Jones, continually flatten the back. The scouts felt that

Jones was not a polished player, that even his three-point stance was awkward, but they were impressed by his raw power. With lots of coaching, they decided, Jones might develop into a pro star. They recommended that the Rams draft him, and the Rams did.

Deacon says of his first days at training camp in 1961: "I found out I didn't know a thing. I was clumsy. When blockers would come straight at me, I was helpless. But I was real hungry. I had made up my mind that this was my one chance and I was going to give it my best shot. If I didn't make it in football, where would I go, what would I do? You don't get anything in life without working and sacrificing and suffering for it. I just literally took hold of the one rung on the ladder that was open to me and hauled myself up."

Deacon listened and practiced and learned. At the end of training camp he was told he'd earned a place on the squad, as a substitute. Then, right before the '61 opener, one of the Rams' first-string defensive ends, Gene Brito, was hospitalized. Jones replaced him and remained a starting end all season.

For three years, as he continued to learn, he was an inconsistent player. Then, in 1964, he began to play spectacularly in game after game. He was picked for the 1964 All-Pro second team. In 1965 he played greater than ever and won a position on the All-Pro first team.

The Rams finished last in 1965, but their defensive line was first rate. Roger Brown had not yet joined the team, and the defensive line consisted of Jones (260 pounds) and Lundy (260 pounds) at the ends, and Olsen (276 pounds) and Roosevelt Grier (285 pounds) at the tackles. All of these men were about six and a half feet tall. When fans began to call them The Fearsome Foursome, the players were delighted. "We are indeed fearsome," Grier said one day. "We are so tall that when we stand at the scrimmage line or go running in with our arms up, the quarterback needs a stepladder to see his receivers. We are so heavy we would flatten a Cadillac if we climbed on the roof."

"And we are so fast — me in particular," said Deacon "that there isn't enough room to get away from us."

The next year the Rams had a new coach, George Allen. And with a better balanced defense and some offensive power, the Rams leaped from last place to third. Then came 1967 and the Coastal Division championship. Deacon made the All-Pro first team both years. In 1967 he was only twenty-nine years old. He seemed certain to continue starring, and perhaps to prove himself the greatest defensive lineman ever.

"Gino Marchetti was one of my idols," Merlin Olsen said one day, talking about the man long rated the finest defensive end in NFL history. "But physically Marchetti was no match for Jones. You'll just have to rate the Deac over Marchetti after this season. You can't believe Deac's quickness and speed. Even when you're playing next to him. It's really quite frustrating. You'll have a good shot at the ball carrier when all of a sudden, whap, Jones is sitting on him."

Always, people have been in awe of Deacon's physical gifts — his speed, his strength, his size. He himself once said that "being big never made me self-conscious. I was never the bully on the block either. I didn't have to be. Guys look at me; they don't want to pick fights with me. I don't look for fights except on the football field. Guys run away from me there. Not the blockers — the quarterbacks. But I catch them.

"Those quarterbacks are always running away from me," Deacon said, laughing. "You know, you'd think they were scared of me."

The Galloping Ghost

IT seems incredible. Today most professional teams play only fourteen games in a whole season, but once a pro team played eight games in twelve days. The year was 1925, and the team was the Chicago Bears. The Bears did it to show off a dazzling halfback named Red Grange.

In those days pro football did not attract big crowds. Pro teams usually had only fifteen players on the entire squad, and since the teams didn't sell many tickets and didn't make much money, they sometimes couldn't even afford to carry as many as fifteen. It was college football that attracted the crowds and commanded the nation's attention. And the best college football player in the land in 1925 was Red Grange. Not since Jim Thorpe, in fact, had any college football player been as big a hero.

So the instant that the 1925 college season

ended, George Halas, coach and owner of the Bears, signed Red Grange to a contract. There was no NFL draft in 1925, and there were no rules preventing a pro team from using a player in the same season he'd played college ball. Halas decided to get Grange into action immediately. "There are millions of people who haven't had a chance to see Grange play this year and want to," Halas reasoned. "We'll give them a chance. And we just might make enough money and attract enough attention to get pro football rolling."

On Thanksgiving Day, 1925, Grange played his first pro game. He didn't play spectacularly but he did draw 36,000 people into Chicago's Wrigley Field, and so many of them stormed the field afterward to see him close up that he needed a police escort to get to the clubhouse. Three days later, in front of a crowd of 26,000, he performed more typically. Running with fluttering feet and dancer's balance, dodging tacklers to get free, and sprinting like a quarter horse once he was free, he gained roughly 150 yards in three quarters and led the Bears to a 14–13 victory over the Columbus Tigers.

Then Grange's work really began. Barnstorming through the nation, the Bears played those eight games in twelve days.

They sold out in St. Louis and drew 35,000 people in Philadelphia. In New York, 65,-000 paid to see Grange. When the tickets sold out, thousands more crashed in through the gates. After that it was Washington, Boston, Pittsburgh, Detroit, and finally back to Chicago. Almost everywhere Grange put on the kind of show that was expected of him. "Grange runs as a shadow flits and drifts and darts, with almost no effort," the sports columnist Grantland Rice wrote. "There is no gathering of muscles for an extra lunge. There is only the effortless, ghostlike weave and glide . . . with a change of pace that can come to a dead stop and pick up instant speed."

Grange earned fifty thousand dollars for his two weeks' work, and as Halas had hoped, he got pro football rolling. From then on the game that fans had ignored would keep growing and growing.

Grange came to pro football when he was twenty-two years old. He was born in Pennsylvania in 1903. When he was five his mother died, and Red moved with his father and brother to Wheaton, Illinois. His father became chief of police in Wheaton, and Red spent his boyhood there — except for one year, when he was fifteen.

That one year Red — or Harold as he was

properly called — lived on an uncle's farm. It was a tough life. Red would get up at dawn, work until school time, then bicycle two miles to class. In the afternoon he'd bicycle back to the farm and work until dark. The muscles on his 140-pound body began to swell and harden, and when he returned to Wheaton he was so strong that he won a dollar from the town iceman by lifting a seventy-five-pound cake of ice onto his shoulder. The iceman was so impressed that he gave Red a job.

Working on the ice truck one day, Red fell and slipped under the back wheel. Speeding on, the truck rolled right over his left thigh. Doctors thought the leg would have to be amputated, but it began to heal, and after four weeks in a hospital bed Red was out of danger. He recovered quickly enough to score 36 touchdowns and kick 39 extra points for the high school football team that autumn.

In his three seasons with the Wheaton high school varsity, Red scored 75 touchdowns and kicked 82 extra points for a career total of 532 points. From there he went to the University of Illinois. In his first varsity game he broke loose for touchdown runs of 35, 65, and 12 yards. "Grange has shown remarkable speed, dodging, hip shift, change of pace," someone wrote. "And when he is caught by several tacklers, the man simply

puts on steam and drives and whirls ahead,
leaving a wake of would-be tacklers strewn
in his path." Red was spectacular through
the season. He earned an All-America rating,
and was the man most responsible for Illinois' undefeated record.

That summer he returned to Wheaton and
the ice wagon. One day a publicity man for
a vaudeville show came by with a photog-
rapher and asked Red to pose with one of his
showgirls. Red did, holding a cake of ice on
his shoulder. The photograph of the All-
America football player and the beauty
queen was then printed in newspapers
around the country, and Red became known
everywhere as "The Wheaton Iceman." As a
result, even people who normally just
skimmed the sports pages lingered over the
name of Red Grange.

As the 1924 season drew near, all of Illinois' forthcoming opponents had the same
game plan: "To win, stop Grange." Big linemen were gearing up to smash the 166-
pound tailback; coaches were shaping special
strategy. And no one was more concerned
with stopping Grange than Coach "Hurry
Up" Yost of Michigan.

In 1923 both Illinois and Michigan had
been undefeated. This year they were to

meet on October 18. The winner, everyone predicted, would most certainly move on to be the Big Ten champ — possibly the national champion as well. Clearly the Michigan-Illinois game would be the season's biggest.

Yost had begun preparing for the game back in the summer by telling sportswriters that he was certain Michigan could throttle Grange. "Mr. Grange," Yost had said, "will be a carefully watched man every time he takes the ball. There will be just about eleven clean, hard Michigan tacklers headed for him at the same time. I know he is a great runner, but great runners usually have the hardest time gaining ground when met by special preparation."

Yost knew that everyone, including Red, read just about everything the sportswriters wrote. Yost was trying to bring up his players' confidence and dampen Red's. But Bob Zuppke, the Illinois coach, had some strategy of his own. He made certain Red saw every newspaper story in which Yost boasted about how Michigan would stop "The Wheaton Iceman." The angrier Red got, Zuppke figured, the more determined he'd be to show up Michigan. And Zuppke was sure he knew Red better than Yost did. Yost's words would not worry Red, Zuppke decided. They would simply make him try harder.

Zuppke also had Red work on some special strategy of his own. He would have Red practice running in a special sideline to sideline pattern. Red would start around right end, speed toward the right sideline, then cut diagonally across to the left sideline, move straight ahead for a moment, and then zoom back to the right sideline. Once Red mastered the pattern, Zuppke set a trap.

The trap began in the Illinois opener against Nebraska. All through that game Red never used his new pattern. He didn't even swerve and dart in the middle of the field the way he had the previous season. Instead, he would swing around end, get over to sideline, and run straight ahead. Although Illinois won the game, Grange gained very few yards. Nebraska had very little trouble simply knocking him out of bounds as he ran straight ahead along the sideline.

The next week, as Illinois beat Butler, Red ran the same way — straight ahead along the sideline — and again he was stopped easily. Yost's scouts observed both games and handed in their reports. Reading them, the Michigan coach was certain he'd be able to stop Red. In fact, he decided, he wasn't going to tell his kickers to keep the ball away from Red. He wanted them to do exactly the opposite. He wanted Red to run with the ball as early in the game as possible, so that the Michigan tacklers could smash Red time after time and demoralize Illinois. "All we have to do," Yost told his team, "is charge straight down that sideline and knock him out of bounds. All he's been doing is running straight ahead."

More than 67,000 people jammed into the Illinois stadium on October 18, 1924. It was the largest crowd ever to attend a game in the Midwest in those days. Michigan kicked off and, true to Yost's strategy, the ball floated right to Red on his own five-yard line. Red caught it and cut to the right sideline, and the Michigan tacklers, following instructions, all plowed after him. He was right where they expected him to be.

But only for an instant. Suddenly, as the Michigan tacklers swarmed in, Red put his new pattern to work. He swung sharply to his left and crossed the whole field. At the left sideline he ran straight ahead for 20 yards, then, as the Michigan players crossed over, cut back to the right sideline and into the end zone. Illinois led 6–0.

At the bench Yost decided it was all a fluke. He wanted Red to get the ball again, as soon as possible, so Michigan could mash him. With the option of kicking off or receiving, Michigan chose to kick off.

Again the ball came to Red, and this time he was stopped on the Illinois 20. Illinois presently had to punt, then held Michigan and got the ball back on the 30. On first down Illinois gained three yards, moving to its 33. On second down Red settled into his tailback's stance, took the snap from center, and weaved around left end to the left sideline. Trapped there, he reversed his field and zigzagged to the right sideline. All the Michigan tacklers had moved to the left with him, and only one of them — the safety — could cut to the right fast enough to get close to him. Racing to the right sideline, Red faked with his hip, suddenly swung left again, and, as the safety clutched at handfuls of air, raced into the end zone.

A few minutes later Red had the ball again. He turned his right end on the Illinois 44 and started down the right sideline. Once more the Michigan tacklers were all over there with him, so he cut back to the left, broke free, and zoomed for a touchdown. Soon after that he took off from his own 45-yard line, ran his crisscrossing pattern again, and scored his fourth touchdown. The game was only twelve minutes old.

Dazzling running patterns made Red Grange's name famous. He darted and dodged like a weaving shadow. Once he made four touchdowns in twelve minutes!

No player has ever put together a more fantastic twelve minutes. And Red wasn't through. In the third quarter he ran 12 yards for another touchdown, and in the fourth he passed 18 yards for still another. And Illinois won 39–14. Red had touchdown runs of 95, 67, 56, 45, and 12 yards; he had gained 402 yards in 21 carries, and he had completed six passes for 78 yards. "It was Grange's good fortune," Ed Linn once wrote, "to play his greatest games on precisely those days when the eyes of the whole football world were focused directly upon him. But, you are bound to ask, is that really luck, or is it the very definition of greatness?"

Clearly, Red was an amazing football player, and as a person — well, "the best way to describe Red Grange as a person,"Linn wrote, "is to say that none of his teammates ever seemed to have the slightest resentment about all the publicity he got in college or all the money he took down in the pros. He was always very popular with teammates and opposition alike."

As tired as his ball carrying made him — and he usually carried the ball on three out of every four plays — "Red would still go all out to block for the others when their numbers were called," Linn wrote. "And he was an excellent blocker. He was also the kind of guy who would bounce up after a particularly shattering tackle and tell the tackler in honest admiration, 'That's the way to hit 'em.' "

They didn't shatter Grange too often though, not in 1924. He went on from the Michigan game to gain a total of 1,164 yards rushing and 534 passing for the season. In 1925 he gained 1,213 yards running and 119 passing. In all, when Illinois had completed the 1925 season, Red had a career record of 4,280 yards gained — 3,637 on the ground, 643 in the air — and 31 touchdowns. He also had a new nickname, one which truly described his football style: "The Galloping Ghost." When Red joined the Bears for that grueling twelve-game pro football tour, fans already knew him as The Galloping Ghost.

When Red had galloped through the tour with the Bears, he went to Hollywood to make a movie. The money he made with the Bears, with the movie, and with various endorsements mounted and mounted. Within months he and his manager, a man named C. C. Pyle, had half a million dollars.

They also had an idea. Since the crowds had come to see Grange, they reasoned, the crowds would continue to come no matter

what team he played for. He didn't need the
Bears or any existing pro team, so why not
ask the NFL for permission to start a new
team — a team starring Grange and owned
by Grange and Pyle?

They asked, and the NFL said no. So
Grange and Pyle started their own league.
Red took over the new league's New York
team and played for it through the 1926 season. As good as he was, though, the new
league didn't make it. The New York team
drew big crowds, but none of the others did.
At the end of the 1926 season the league
folded, and the NFL changed its mind. Permission was given for Red to bring his New
York team into the National Football
League, even though the NFL had another
team, the Giants, in that city.

In an exhibition game against the Bears
before the 1927 season, Red carried into the
line, tried to twist into the open, and caught
his cleats in the ground. Just then the Bears'
big center, George Trafton, smashed into
him. Literally stuck in the ground, Red was
yanked backward with a searing pressure on
his legs. His knee was twisted so badly that
he limped the rest of that season and couldn't
play at all during the next season. Without
Red, the New York team disbanded in 1928.

"I was just another halfback after that injury," Red once said. But he was wrong. He no longer could shift directions as artfully as before, but he could still run fast. And since he had always been a complete football player, he could still block and tackle and catch as well as any back in the league. He could pass, too, and defend against passes. In fact few defensive backs have ever had his skill at swooping in on a receiver and swooping away with the football.

Red rejoined the Bears in 1929 and presently became the first man in motion out of the T-formation, a maneuver that allowed him to wheel toward the sideline from his halfback position before the ball was snapped and then shoot out into the secondary to catch passes. Through the years he caught enough passes, made enough long runs, and broke up enough plays to earn a rating as one of the most valuable players in the league. In 1932 he was the first-team halfback on the first NFL all-star team ever picked. "He lacked the maneuverability of the old Grange," Tex Maule once wrote, "but he served the Bears brilliantly." And Red did all this while he was wearing a special brace of elastic and steel on his knee.

Red played his last game on January 27,

1935. It was an exhibition against the Giants, and deep into it Red sprung free at his own 20. He was in the open and moving — to the 30, the 40. He was at midfield, with a clear route ahead. And suddenly he was flat on his face, caught from behind. Red was thirty-two years old then, and his knee had been getting worse game after game. He had once scored four touchdowns in twelve minutes. Another time he had run for 363 yards on a field soaked with mud. His running and reputation had turned pro football into a prosperous business. But now he had been caught from behind by a 230-pound *lineman!* It was time to be retired and be remembered for the days when any fan would have laughed out loud if someone had suggested the possibility of a 230-pound lineman racing up from yards behind and catching The Galloping Ghost.